How to Manage your Arts, Humanities and Social Science Degree

Palgrave Study Guides

A Handbook of Writing for Engineers   *Joan van Emden*
Authoring a PhD Thesis   *Patrick Dunleavy*
Effective Communication for Arts and Humanities Students
   Joan van Emden and Lucinda Becker
Effective Communication for Science and Technology   *Joan van Emden*
How to Manage your Arts, Humanities and Social Science Degree
   Lucinda Becker
How to Write Better Essays   *Bryan Greetham*
Key Concepts in Politics   *Andrew Heywood*
The Mature Student's Guide to Writing   *Jean Rose*
The Postgraduate Research Handbook   *Gina Wisker*
Professional Writing   *Sky Marsen*
Research Using IT   *Hilary Coombes*
The Student's Guide to Writing   *John Peck and Martin Coyle*
The Study Skills Handbook   *Stella Cottrell*
Studying Economics   *Brian Atkinson and Susan Johns*
Studying History (second edition)   *Jeremy Black and Donald M. MacRaild*
Studying Mathematics and its Applications   *Peter Kahn*
Studying Psychology   *Andrew Stevenson*
Teaching Study Skills and Supporting Learning   *Stella Cottrell*

Palgrave Study Guides: Literature

General Editors: John Peck and Martin Coyle

How to Begin Studying English Literature (second edition)
   Nicholas Marsh
How to Study a Jane Austen Novel (second edition)   *Vivien Jones*
How to Study Chaucer (second edition)   *Rob Pope*
How to Study a Charles Dickens Novel   *Keith Selby*
How to Study Foreign Languages   *Marilyn Lewis*
How to Study an E. M. Forster Novel   *Nigel Messenger*
How to Study James Joyce   *John Blades*
How to Study Linguistics   *Geoffrey Finch*
How to Study Modern Drama   *Tony Curtis*
How to Study Modern Poetry   *Tony Curtis*
How to Study a Novel (second edition)   *John Peck*
How to Study a Poet (second edition)   *John Peck*
How to Study a Renaissance Play   *Chris Coles*
How to Study Romantic Poetry (second edition)   *Paul O'Flinn*
How to Study a Shakespeare Play   *John Peck and Martin Coyle*
How to Study Television   *Keith Selby and Ron Cowdery*
Linguistic Terms and Concepts   *Geoffrey Finch*
Literary Terms and Criticism (third edition)   *John Peck and Martin Coyle*
Practical Criticism   *John Peck and Martin Coyle*

How to Manage your Arts, Humanities and Social Science Degree

Lucinda Becker

First published 2003 by
PALGRAVE MACMILLAN
Houndmills, Basingstoke, Hampshire RG21 6XS and
175 Fifth Avenue, New York, N.Y. 10010
Companies and representatives throughout the world

PALGRAVE MACMILLAN is the global academic imprint of the Palgrave Macmillan division of St. Martin's Press, LLC and of Palgrave Macmillan Ltd. Macmillan® is a registered trademark in the United States, United Kingdom and other countries. Palgrave is a registered trademark in the European Union and other countries.

ISBN 1-4039-0054-X paperback

This book is printed on paper suitable for recycling and made from fully managed and sustained forest sources.

A catalogue record for this book is available from the British Library.

10 9 8 7 6 5 4 3 2 1
12 11 10 09 08 07 06 05 04 03

Printed and bound in Great Britain by Creative Print and Design (Wales), Ebbw Vale.

Contents

Acknowledgements

I would like to thank all my colleagues and students who have helped in the shaping of this book; my gratitude also to Alan Stacey, who took time out of his undergraduate studying in order to offer his contribution.

My special thanks to Paul McColm, who managed his own degree with such aplomb and has, since our time at university together, been generous in sharing his experiences and insights with me.

My thanks to Anastasia and Felicity Becker who patiently and meticulously helped to prepare the index.

The author and publisher would like to thank the following for permission to reproduce copyright material: the first two stanzas of 'Song' from *The Poems of John Donne*, edited by Sir Herbert J.C. Grierson, published by Oxford University Press (1942). Reproduced by permission of the literary executors of Sir Herbert J.C. Grierson.

1 Introduction

▶ Your degree

This is a book about choices; not just the obvious choices you already know that you will have to make at university (which courses to take, which books to read) but also those choices that you may not yet have thought about (which lectures to attend, which career to choose). This is not a conventional study guide; there are many useful books available that will help you to write an essay, study a work of literature or present at a seminar. What this book is all about is the management of your degree, the ways in which you can make sure that you have the best time possible and achieve the right result by the end of your course. The book does not, for example, teach you how to skim read a reference book, but it will tell you how to choose which reference books to read and which to discard. It does not aim to teach you how to write an essay, but it will show you how to plan your time so that you can get the essay in by the due date without having a nervous breakdown in the process. The book also helps with those areas of student life that are not covered in traditional study skills guides, such as how to make your money last to the end of your course, how to cope with peer pressure and how to make the most of your tutors.

There was a time when being an undergraduate was essentially a passive experience. You were presented with a fairly rigid course structure and you worked your way through it until you reached your final examinations, which you hoped to pass. In this way it did not feel that different from pre-university studying. Students have always had to produce essays, contribute to seminars and pass examinations, but now they are increasingly proactive about the experience of being an undergraduate, often having to choose between competing modules, giving professional-level presentations and working under a variety of assessment conditions. They also have to juggle the demands of their studying, a social life and the financial constraints placed upon them. You are in what might be called an 'asymmetrical bargaining position'. You want to be at university, many courses are oversubscribed and you are probably aware that another student would have taken your place had you not taken it up. You have competed to get here and have succeeded, so you will probably feel relieved to be on your course, at your university. On the other hand, whilst universities are centres of excellence for research, they are also teaching institutions that must meet the needs of their students. You can feel confident that you have a right to be here, just as your university has a right to expect that you will undertake the task before you with a level of commitment and (they hope) enthusiasm.

This may seem like a fairly straightforward bargain: you work well, the university gives you a degree and everyone is happy. What makes the bargain asymmetrical, especially in its early stages, is that they do not know everything about you and you will not know everything about them. Your department can be fairly certain that it has made the right choice. They know about your academic achievements and have references about you. However, what they may not know, for example, is that, although you write very well, you are anxious about speaking out in a seminar, or that although you can get through reading lists, you take forever to plough through each book. Perhaps you have to work for cash whilst you study or maybe your parents are moving abroad, making access to a library in the vacations problematic. These are the sort of things that they will need to learn about you. What you may not know about are all the aspects of university life that did not feature in your decision-making process when you made your choices about where to study. It may be, for example, that you assumed that assessment would be primarily through examinations, but your chosen courses are assessed exclusively by coursework, which you find difficult, or perhaps you are having more trouble than you anticipated finding accommodation near the university. Life as an undergraduate is, in this way, a continuing form of negotiation. You will work well, but only when you know what is expected of you and feel in control of the process. The university staff will support you, but can only do this if they know about problems as they arise. This book will help you to negotiate effectively as your degree course progresses. University life is not about 'you' and 'them'; your department will do its utmost to help you, and you can help yourself, and them, by getting to grips with the issues raised in this book. Hurdles can be overcome, your time can be managed effectively, your achievement level can rise. All this, and more, is possible for every student.

The advice offered within this book is inevitably generalised, offered to help you to negotiate all the differing aspects of your degree. Its aim is to share with you all the facets of university life, but one word of warning is necessary: your department is the best place to go in order to get the definitive facts about your life at university. This book will reveal to you the ways in which you can move forward and maximise your potential and the help that is available to you if things go wrong, but you will still need to check with your personal tutor, departmental handbook or subject secretary about specific points and your own university's regulations. You may never have any contact with the regulatory bodies within your university, but these exist in order to enforce the regulations of the university, adjudicate on problem situations and listen to appeals about results and disciplinary action. Make a point of at least getting to grips with the rudimentary points of your university's regulations: they are usually clearly explained within the available literature and there will be a system in place to cover almost every eventuality.

▶ The structure of your degree programme

Perhaps the most significant change in higher education in recent years is the way in which degrees have become largely modular in structure. As a result, students enjoy a more flexible degree package and want to get the best possible result in a degree that may link more directly to their career choice than in the past. Modular degrees are the ideal way to ensure that students study and enjoy those courses that really interest them and allow them to study not just their core subjects, but also peripheral subjects that will give them pleasure and in which they can succeed. The downside to modular degrees is that they can be a bit confusing, and you might feel that one wrong move could wreck your degree. You can also be left feeling that there is too much choice, that you want to do it all. There is no need to worry; as well as reading this book, you will get support from your department as to how to make the right modular choices, whether you choose on the basis of interest alone, to suit your timetable or fit in with your preference for certain modes of assessment.

Whatever choices you make about the exact profile of your degree, your course of study will cost you a good deal of time, money and effort, and you will want to get it right. Anxiety is one of the greatest inhibitors of performance. If you are worried about what is expected of you, feel pressurised by a peer group which is not helping you or constantly concerned about how you are going to survive financially, you will not work effectively. There are as many different students at university, from as many different backgrounds and cultures, as there are individuals in any other area of life. You will see undergraduates around you who seem to shine in every task, are involved in several university societies and always seem to be able to produce answers in seminars with confidence and apparently no effort. You will also see, if you look a little more closely, students who are bewildered, struggling to keep up or experiencing problems in specific areas of student life. Whichever type of student you are, this book can be of use to you. What you do not want for yourself is to be going home at the end of your first term feeling exhausted, with no cash left and no clear idea as to whether you are getting it right or wrong. This could leave you questioning whether you should even be at university, when in reality you are doing no worse than most of your fellow undergraduates. The first aim of this guide is to help you to cope with the initial stages of life as an undergraduate.

For many students, the first two terms at university will differ radically from the rest of their course. You may find that this time is spent covering the fundamentals of your subject or subjects, particularly if you are taking a degree in more than one subject. However, for most students, these terms give them an opportunity to study subjects outside their core courses, perhaps very different subjects from those that they will be studying for the rest of their time at university. The first stage of your degree may see you tackling a subject that you will never study again and this is an exciting prospect. You will also be creating a social life and perhaps finding a part-time job. Chapter 4 will tell you how to make the most of the first six weeks of your life at university, whilst Chapter 5 will help you to decide between the options that are open to you. Being able to choose from a variety of courses as your degree progresses is a key feature of your undergraduate experience, but there are two things to bear in mind as you read this book and make those choices. Firstly, you do not need to have a firm plan in mind when you enter university. You have probably chosen a course because of the modules that it offers, but make sure that you remain open to new possibilities as they arise. No guide to a department can include every possible choice that might be made available to students, so reconsidering your degree profile regularly is vital if you are to make the most of your time.

The second point to bear in mind is that it is rarely too late to change your mind. Of course, if you are already halfway through a two-term module when you decide that you hate it, it is probably not possible (or worth your while) for you to change. The advice offered in this book will help you to understand what has gone wrong and will point you in the right direction so that the course becomes bearable. However, many students feel trapped when they have no need to feel this way. You might choose a module in all good faith, believing that it will suit your needs, be of interest to you and in which you can succeed. You begin the module and decide that it is wrong for you, perhaps because you misunderstood the information given to you, or because the course or method of assessment has changed. There are a multitude of reasons why you might decide that a module (or even, as can sometimes happen, your whole degree) is wrong for you, and this book will help you to focus your thinking, decide what to do and then make the necessary changes with the support of your department and tutor.

▶ The wider aspects of your degree course

Humanities and Social Science degrees are rewarding because they are not designed exclusively to get you into a job and keep you there. If you are taking a highly specialised or vocational degree, you may well know what career you are aiming for even before you get to university, but for most Humanities and Social Science undergraduates university is an adventure in itself; ideas about a career will be in your thoughts, but not completely fixed. This gives you the advantage of knowing that you can develop your career ideas as your course progresses, aware that your degree will be of help to you in many areas of work. It is perhaps with this in mind that Humanities and Social Science degree programmes tend to be very wide in scope and flexible in approach. You might go to university to study Politics and find yourself doing some work within the Law department, or you might take a degree in French but decide to include a module from the Italian department.

Universities work hard to help you to maximise your skills base. Of course you are here to study your core subject or subjects, but the aim of a degree is to prepare you for life, to train your mind to work effectively in situations that are entirely unrelated to your degree. It will sometimes be difficult, when you are dashing to keep up with your course, to appreciate that you are acquiring new skills, but there is no doubt that this is exactly what will be happening. Whatever your subject, you will be learning to manage your time, read critically, analyse opinions and information that are being presented to you, form an argument logically, communicate it effectively and present your thoughts articulately. You will also be familiarising yourself with the logistics of team building, acquiring leadership qualities and learning the techniques of presentation that are so important to employers. These things do not happen by chance: universities deliberately organise the workload of students so as to allow these qualities to develop and you will have ample opportunity to work at these skills and find ways to demonstrate them. If you are unclear about what is expected of you or unhappy with your course or your performance, you will find that your route to mastering these skills is hampered. It is the task of this book to clear the way for you, to allow you to achieve your full potential in the time that you have at university.

The formal structure of your degree, the courses that you take, are only the starting point of the experiences that you will have at university. Some of the other features of taking a degree may not yet have occurred to you. You might, for example, be expected to give a formal, professional-level presentation, or work on your own, supported by your tutor, on a piece of research. You might be working to earn some money as you study, or become involved in a student society. You are increasingly likely to be required to undertake a module of career research and assessment and your department, school or faculty may offer a range of further opportunities, from work placements to time spent studying abroad. All these options are discussed in this book and they all represent vitally important aspects of your undergraduate experience. This guide is designed to remove the unnecessary pressures of uncertainty and confusion, so that you can begin your degree in a positive frame of mind and continue to work effectively, without burdening yourself unnecessarily, leaving you time to explore and make the most of every opportunity.

▶ How to use this book

So you have to make choices, decisions that will affect your time at university, perhaps fundamentally. Universities expect a higher level of sophistication from their students than ever before, yet you might not always feel equipped to make these choices. That is why this book exists: to help you to maximise your potential during your degree and help when things feel as if they are getting out of hand. Things can seem to be disastrous when you start to believe that you are losing control of your time and your studying: the reading list is just too long, essay submission dates clash or you feel that you have missed a whole chunk of learning that everyone else seems completely confident about. That is when you need to sit back, take stock and decide how to handle the situation.

University life can seem very strange, particularly at the beginning, and miles away from your experience as a pre-university student. If you are a mature student, who has completed an access course or come to university straight from a career, life as an undergraduate can be even more disorientating. By reading this book you will get a feel for what is expected of you and what you can expect from your university. Although many university departments make great efforts to familiarise their students with the ways in which they will be studying, it can sometimes feel as if there is something missing, a secret that you need to discover before you can truly settle into your new life. What your department demands of you is obvious to the university; it may be far less clear to you, despite the handbooks and guides that are produced by the university. If you are to make the most of your time at university, you will need to familiarise yourself with the system as soon as possible. Spending hours (perhaps days) worrying about a reading list, how assessment works or how you are going to get enough cash to survive is time wasted. Reading this book is a far easier (and less painful) way of ensuring that you quickly become a confident, and therefore successful, undergraduate.

The skills that this book will help you to master will be relevant throughout your course. As you read through the book, you will find that it will support you during the whole of your time as an undergraduate. From getting started and making the right choices in the first six weeks or so of university, it then tackles the issue of further options later in your course. All the practicalities of your studying are covered, including reading lists, means of assessment, lectures, tutorials and seminars. Chapter 6 deals with life beyond studying, including how to survive financially, how to network and use peer pressure to your advantage and where to go to make the most of university social life. Chapter 7 is devoted to how you can cope if things begin to go wrong for you, offering you clear, practical guidance on how to make things right again. The final chapter takes you beyond your degree by helping you with the challenge of getting a job when you leave university.

Your life as an undergraduate is not going to be beset by problems. This is not an academic obstacle course, laden with impossible hurdles that have been deliberately placed in your way. For much of your time at university you will sail along, feeling confident about your work and enjoying what you are doing. The secret to success is eliminating problems before they arise. As you work through each chapter of this book, you will be getting ahead of the game. Even before you are faced with an assessed essay, you will feel confident about how to approach it. If you are confused by a lecture, you will know how to deal with it. If you are expected to give a presentation, you will not be daunted by the prospect. You will also be able to keep in mind that there is a life after university and you will be preparing for this. This guide will offer you reassurance, not just about the practicalities of taking a degree, but about your own experience of life at university. You may find yourself, on occasion, feeling muddled about what you are doing, or confused by concepts or theories, but knowing that everyone else feels this way at times, realising that your feelings of insecurity (as well as your elation at successes) are entirely normal, can be a big help. This book aims to assure you that your reaction to this new life is quite normal and that difficulties, should they arise, are both common and often relatively easy to overcome.

By the time you are well into your studying you may not have the time, or perhaps the inclination, to reread whole chapters of this book, but it might be useful to check that you are still on the right lines, or remind yourself of how best to approach a new situation. It is for this reason that each chapter closes with a 'spot guide'. The spot guide gives you each key point of the chapter in one sentence, allowing you to confirm to yourself that you are clear about what you are doing, or prompting you to reread a section of the chapter in order to get to grips with a situation in more detail. After your initial reading, you may have to go back to only one or two chapters in detail, but by checking the spot guide you will have the benefit of knowing that you have mastered all the management aspects of each chapter. Towards the end of your degree, your experience will have been reflected in each chapter of the book and you will be ready to work with the guidance in the final chapter as you move into your chosen career.

When stressed out students are asked what is wrong with them, they often give the vaguest of answers. They think that they might be homesick, university is not living up to their expectations or they are not clever enough, quick enough or sussed enough to cope with university life. It is easy for those who are trying to help to see them as inarticulate, unable to be helped effectively because what is wrong seems so intangible. Yet very often the problem is not that the students are being unhelpful, or refusing to help themselves, but that they really do not know what is making them unhappy, or preventing them from getting the grades that are expected of them. Usually they are confused and demoralised precisely because they cannot put a finger on what is going awry. If you find yourself thinking that there is just too much work being piled onto you, you need to discover why you feel like this. It is possible, of course, that there really is too much work being handed out to you in one term (it happens), but it is more likely that you are not successfully managing your time as an undergraduate, perhaps because you are working to earn money at the same time, you have made what are the wrong course choices for you or you are unclear about what is expected of you.

Undergraduates are not naturally vague, nor are they lazy, but they do need to be clear about what is going on. You will find that each chapter of this book opens with a troubleshooting guide that is designed to help you if you feel that things are running out of control. By checking the troubleshooting guide, you will be able to identify the problem that is at the root of your troubles and you will find help within the chapter to guide you through that aspect of your degree. It may not solve all your problems, but identifying the source of your difficulty will take you halfway towards solving it, and there are plenty of pointers in each chapter as to where to go next to get help. You will find that, in most cases, your problem will be solved simply by understanding what is going on. Once you know the difference between a seminar paper and a seminar presentation, for example, you will understand what is expected of you in each circumstance. If you are clear about how to use reading lists, you will relax and benefit from what they have to offer. Once your options become clear to you, you will get on with the task of making the most of them.

The pressure is on students like never before. You will probably have come to university via a system that required you to perform well in SATs, GCSEs, A and AS levels or within another pre-university course. You have had to be focused on passing examinations, getting the grades and working exactly as you are expected to do in order to achieve. This may have resulted in the best ever pass rates at all levels, but it has left students to face life as undergraduates with a preconception that nothing else matters but passing each module and excelling in each examination. These things are important, of course, but other areas of university life are important also. In recent years more and more students ask me, as soon as we begin a course of study, exactly what they have to do in order to pass the examination at the end. We may be looking at the most wonderful piece of English Literature, or exploring a fascinating management topic, but students can still feel that they have no time to ponder the wider implications of what they are doing. Passing the examination, getting a good degree, is everything, to the exclusion of all else. If you use this book in all its aspects, I hope that you will have the time, free from worrying, to look around you and enjoy what you are doing, appreciate the pleasures of university and make the most of your life as an undergraduate.

People will tell you that these are 'the best years of your life'. This is all very well in retrospect (and, for most people, it is true) but it is difficult to see this if you are drowning under a sea of books, or slaving over a hot computer producing three essays in one week. If you are able to manage your degree programme effectively, and this book will help you to do that, you will at least be able to look up long enough to enjoy your time at university and appreciate why these might, indeed, be the best years of your life.

2 Getting Started

Troubleshooting guide

Read this chapter for help in the following areas:

- if you are not sure that you are doing the right degree course for you or suspect that you need to make some changes
- if you are not clear about how to make the transition from earlier methods of studying to undergraduate ways of working
- if you are confused about how to make connections between modules, texts, ideas, theories and ideologies
- if you have trouble grasping the 'big ideas' involved in undergraduate study
- if you are concerned about how you will be assessed, and how to make the assessment procedure work for you
- if you are not sure what is meant by the terms 'seminar', 'dissertation', 'assessed coursework' and 'viva', or the differences between a seminar paper and a seminar presentation

▶ The relationship between undergraduate study and your earlier forms of studying

There are four common ways in which a student might choose a degree subject or subjects; you will probably fall into one of these categories:

1. You might simply be carrying on with whatever subject or subjects were your 'best' subjects at school or college.
2. You might have had little choice about your subject: if you wanted to go to a particular university, for example, or if you did not do as well as you had expected in your pre-university examinations.

3. You might have chosen a subject with one eye firmly on the future and based your choice on whatever course you thought would best help you into your chosen career.
4. You might have chosen a subject on no other grounds than that it appeals to you.

When you came to fill out your UCAS form, it probably all seemed a bit theoretical. You can feel as if the process is rather unreal: you are choosing a university, and a subject, on not a great deal of evidence, and suddenly it is all real, it is all happening, and you are here, at university, studying a subject that less than a year ago was no more than a choice amongst several written on a form. If you have taken a gap year, the distance between making a decision and actually being at university studying a subject is, of course, even greater. It is worth taking some time, now that you are at university, to think about which category, or categories, you fall into, as this may have an impact upon your performance, methods of study and overall motivation.

If you are continuing with your 'best' subject, now is the time to think about what made it the 'best'. Was it because you always got good grades? Or because you showed a real flair for several aspects of the subject? Or because your school or college was particularly keen on this field of study? Whatever the reasons for it being chosen as your best choice, you now need to revisit it as a subject, to ascertain what it is about it that you enjoy, and how you see your relationship with your subject developing over the course of your degree. The potential problem for you is that you may not feel that you really chose the subject at all. It is all too easy to assume that you must carry on with a subject because you have achieved good results in your earlier studying, and undergraduates can feel that their subject was actually chosen by their school or college, or their parents. If, upon reflection, you decide that this is the case for you, the first few weeks of your undergraduate course is the best time to work out whether you really want to spend three or four years living with the subject, whether you would rather change course or opt for a combined or joint degree course.

The case is similar if you did less well that you had expected in your pre-university qualifications and so signed up to a course, or a university, that was not your first choice. At first you may just feel relieved to have got into university, or you may be concerned that you have ended up at your second (or third, fourth or fifth) choice of university. However, you will soon discover that you are not alone, that many of your fellow students, for a variety of reasons, have been through the same process as you. You need not feel that you no longer have a choice, or that you simply have to keep your head down and be grateful for your place at university. However you got to be here, you still have the right to choose how you would like your degree to develop, and it is important that you come to feel that your subject really is *your* subject, one that you will be happy to work in for the next three or four years. The chances are that you will decide that, however the subject was chosen, it is the one for you. Universities take great care to try to make their courses as interesting and varied as possible, and you will almost certainly find enough that is of interest in your course to keep you motivated. If you come to realise that this is the best subject for you, the time spent considering it in this way will not have been wasted. You will now be ready to move forward with no qualms about the fundamental reason for being at your university, that is, studying your chosen subject.

However, it is not too late to make changes. It is far better to weigh up the options in the first half term of your undergraduate career and make alterations to your course at that stage, than to struggle on for several terms and then decide that you have made a horrible mistake. It is worth bearing in mind that your course will probably allow for a high degree of flexibility as you progress; you will be asked to make decisions about the exact profile of your degree as you go along, so you need not feel that you are locked into an irrevocable course of study from the very beginning. However, if your gut feeling is that this is not the course for you, if you get bored in every lecture and drag yourself to every seminar, feeling that you are out of your depth or studying with students with whom you feel no connection, then take the plunge and talk to your personal tutor about the problem. This is *your* degree, you are devoting several years of your life to it and it has to be right for you. Tutors are used to finding several students each year at their doors, asking for their degree courses to be modified or changed altogether, so if you find that this is the case for you, do not be afraid to come forward. Sometimes just admitting that there is a problem and talking it over with a tutor can help you to decide that the course is not wrong at all. It may be that simple, practical things are getting in the way of your studying, and by talking about it you will have made a positive step forward and taken ownership of your degree. From then on your life as an undergraduate will be far easier.

Increasingly students choose their degree subjects as part of an overall career plan. A degree is expensive and it is time consuming. Undergraduates devote three or four years to a course of study and, for many, this is only justifiable if the degree is directly relevant to their career choice. If this is the case for you, you are unlikely to lack motivation. You know why you are here and you are going to get on with the task ahead of you. Having said that, there is no reason why you should not maximise the enjoyment and satisfaction that you gain from your course of study. So, whilst you go ahead with your core subject, it is worth keeping an open mind about what else is on offer. You might decide to take one module in another department, or to take up options that are less relevant to your career choice but will make your degree more interesting and engaging. You may also find, as many students do, that your career ideas will change. University provides a great opportunity to scout around and look at fresh career ideas and new course possibilities. If you remain open to new options, both in terms of your career and your course, you will have the satisfaction of knowing, as your work progresses, that you are doing exactly the right thing for you. It is also the case that many of the options available to you within the university but outside your core course, such as additional studying or joining societies or action groups, will not be obvious to you until you settle into university life, but these extra activities can add materially to your CV, so they are always worth investigating.

If you have chosen your degree subject purely because you enjoy it, you are perhaps in the most fortunate position. You are here to explore a subject with which you feel an affinity and you are unlikely to have any hesitation in throwing yourself into the studying. However, even in this case it is worth checking that the profile of your degree course (what modules you can take, how the timetable will work, the availability of the courses publicised as being on offer) is as you thought it would be. By studying the material that your department produces on your degree, you can confirm that this really is the best course for you in all its aspects. You may have to compromise on a course or two but if, having done some research, you feel that the degree is still the right one for you (and this is likely to be the case), you will be ready to go ahead with a full commitment to your undergraduate life.

For some students, their choice of subject is fairly arbitrary, they just want to get an all important degree so as to move on to a successful career. If this is true of you, you can still maximise your opportunities now that you are at university. However you arrived at this point, what lies ahead of you is the best possible chance to extend your knowledge base, develop your skills and enjoy yourself.

▶ The differences between earlier studying and a degree

One of the most common early challenges in managing your degree may well be making the transition from your usual methods of studying and the requirements of an undergraduate course. There is an understandable temptation at the end of your pre-university course to throw away all your notes and forget it all: university life will be entirely different, you feel, and so your old notes will be irrelevant. There is an equally understandable and contradictory urge to retain everything from your pre-university course, the notes, methods of working and approach to your subject. After all, if you have done well enough to get here, the ways of working at school or college should work for you here. The gap between pre-university and undergraduate study can seem huge to some students, whilst others do not expect there to be any differences at all between the two. In fact, in order to manage your degree to greatest effect, you will need to distinguish between the two, retaining what is useful from your previous courses whilst moving on to develop new ways of learning. Of course, many aspects of study will remain the same. You will still be studying a variety of texts and grappling with ideas and theories. You will still be asked to present arguments and reach conclusions. There will still be facts to remember and essays and projects to be completed to a deadline.

However, there are differences and these are worth considering as you begin your course, and as your life as an undergraduate progresses. You will probably be bombarded with reading lists, detailing far more texts than you might have expected, and certainly far more texts than you will ever have time to read in their entirety. You are also likely be asked, particularly in the first two terms, to do a 'whistle-stop tour' through your subject or subjects. The seminars come fast and furiously, you are likely to be studying several subjects, each department will be asking you to perform, and much of what is being expected of you will feel unfamiliar, although in reality it will still be based upon many of the fundamental study skills that you have already mastered. If you are a mature student, it may be some time since you studied in this formal way, and so the sense of disorientation is even greater.

Despite this, all is not lost. If you are to manage your degree, make the most of your time and achieve to the best of your ability, you will have to decide, before all else, where your skills lie. It may be that you are fantastic at remembering dates, names, random facts and quotations; or perhaps you enjoy theories and grasping new concepts. Maybe you read very quickly, or have the knack of writing fluently and authoritatively. Now is the time to review your A level course, or your recent training or learning experiences, and assess both your strengths and those areas where you need to develop your skills further. If you are good at thinking on your feet, seminars will come easily to you, whereas if you are a careful planner and meticulous thinker, you will enjoy having the time to develop your thoughts in essays. The secret to success is to recognise similarities between what you are being asked to do now and what you have done in the past. You may be used to studying a text over several weeks and be horrified to discover that you are to receive just one lecture and one seminar on a text before moving on. At this point, do not panic. The requirements are the same, you will still be asked to read the text, understand it and have ideas about it based upon your own experience and understanding of your subject and the secondary texts that are available to you. You may have spent some time prior to university looking at a political theory and then find that at university it is discussed, dissected and dismissed within one seminar. This does not undervalue the theory, it simply allows you the option of considering it in more detail as you develop it in an essay or for a seminar presentation. Similarly, in Social Science, you may feel panic rising as you are required to study, in some detail and at speed, statistical data with which you are unfamiliar.

The key here is to hold your nerve. You may feel flustered and out on a limb, but your fellow undergraduates will all be feeling like this, to a greater or lesser extent, and you will get used to the pace of work. You will also find that the pressure eases as you become familiar with what is required of you, and as the course develops and you begin to specialise in those areas that interest you most. You will be developing your level of self-discipline, aided by a personal study programme, as outlined in Chapter 3. Once you have recognised your strengths, it is time to take the plunge and try to develop other areas. Nobody is going to do the studying for you, but this book will help you to manage those areas in which you need the greatest help, so that you will feel able to present at a seminar, cope with an enormous reading list and produce an essay in the most effective way possible. In the meantime, do not throw away your school or college notes. You need to move away from being a pre-university student and master new techniques and ways of working, but, as your course develops, you will see the relevance of what you have studied in the past and be surprised at how often your earlier essays and notes can give you clues in your undergraduate work.

▶ Taking a wider view than in your pre-university studying

There are three key differences between pre-university work and undergraduate study. Firstly, there is the timing, the need to keep up with what can seem like an overwhelming workload, particularly in the early stages of your course. The aim of this book is to help you to manage your time and workload so that you can work effectively and enjoy your course. Secondly, there are seminars or presentation groups that may feel very different to the classroom situation with which you are familiar. You are probably used to studying each of your chosen subjects within a stable group in each lesson, whereas at university you may be a member of five or six different seminar groups at any one time and this can be daunting. In fact, this 'mixing and matching' will probably become one of the positive aspects of the course: you will meet a wide range of your fellow undergraduates, have the opportunity to speak out in a variety of situations and, most importantly, if the members of one of your seminar groups are largely silent and entirely boring, the chances are that you will also belong to a more interesting group for another module. Of course, you can always follow the advice in Chapter 5 and make each of your seminars a scintillating experience.

The final and perhaps the most subtle difference between your earlier studying and undergraduate life is the need to think as widely as possible about each text that you are studying, each concept that you are discussing, each study situation with which you are faced. In some ways, mature students have the advantage here. They often bring with them to undergraduate life a vast array of life experience, the advantage of having read widely and a grasp of the connections between subjects. However, each undergraduate can rapidly develop the technique required in order to take the wider view. There are three aspects to this technique:

1. Make sure that you do not abandon anything you have ever learnt. Your pre-university European History course may be relevant to your reading of European novels of the 18th century. Your school or college work placement, or your past career, might have some bearing on your sociological study of women in the workplace. Your school theatre trip to a Chekhov play might aid your understanding of Russian Social History.

2. If you do have an opinion, do not be afraid to voice it, both in seminars and written work. Undergraduate seminars all over the country each week are full of students, many of whom will have great ideas, but who feel hesitant about speaking out or including them in essays. Working at degree level is all about reading, understanding and forming educated opinions based upon what you have read, but it is also, at its best, about you having your own opinions. You will not get it right all the time, of course. There will be occasions when your tutor will point you in another direction but, if you offer an opinion, you will be impressing the lecturers, stimulating debate and, as importantly, saving yourself a lot of time. By venturing an opinion at a seminar, you will get instant feedback, relevant guidance as to where to go next and a highly gratified tutor who will remember your original contribution to the course – always a good thing.

3. Try not to assume that the reading you do for pleasure, the discussions you have in the Student Union bar or the programmes you watch on TV or listen to on the radio have no relevance to your studying. University lecturers are delighted to find graduates who can make relevant and interesting connections between their life outside studying and the subject with which they are engaged, or who can see the connections between different texts, ideas and modules. It is this aspect of undergraduate study that we will consider next.

▶ Making connections between modules, texts, ideas and ideologies

Managing your degree successfully is not always about working harder: it is equally about working smarter. Making relevant connections as you go along is one of the most important aspects of the management of your studying. The choices that you can make in terms of the modules that you take will be discussed in some detail in Chapter 5, where you will discover how to make choices that will achieve maximum results for a reasonable amount of effort. However, in addition to making choices that will be of greatest benefit to you in terms of your degree profile, you will also be able to find unexpected connections between the modules you have chosen that will be of benefit to you as your degree progresses. The secret is to be on the lookout for them. Modules usually extend over at least two terms, and it is useful for all sorts of reasons for you to take a little time, both halfway through and at the end of each module, to assess the key ideas that have been addressed and the texts, theories and ideologies that have been covered. Of course, if a module ends with the submission of coursework or an examination, then you will be undertaking this task anyway. Once you have set out the essential elements in a module, you will be able to compare one module to another, both those within your primary field of study and those within other subjects. The example below sets out how you can then use this to your advantage.

Let's say, for the purposes of this example, that a student is taking three modules, one in Classical Studies, one in English Literature and one in Philosophy. You are most likely to be studying three such disparate subjects in your first year, but the modular form of undergraduate programmes allows students to study widely at all stages of their courses. Within each module, I have listed five key areas that our example student might be exploring:

Classical Studies

The role of poetry in Classical Rome
Theatrical performances in Ancient Greece
The political impact of the performing arts in the Ancient World
The birth of democracy
The teachings of Plato and Socrates

Philosophy

The theory of the self
Plato and Socrates

Ethics
Descartes
John Stuart Mill

English Literature

Hamlet: performance and theory
Comic relief in Shakespeare's plays
Milton: his life and work
The development of the novel
The works of James Joyce

At first glance, this may look like rather a disparate list of ideas and areas of study. A couple of points might hit you immediately, such as the fact that you could use what you have learnt in Classical Studies about the lives of Plato and Socrates in your work in Philosophy. You might also know, from earlier reading, that Milton held strong views about his political role as a poet in a turbulent age, and so a glancing reference back to Classical poets and their political role might boost your essay on Milton. However, the connections go far beyond this, once you really begin to look for them. The following are examples of the potential connections:

- the theory and practice of theatrical performance in Classical Rome could be used to underpin your discussion of modern performances of *Hamlet*
- the political impact of the performing arts in Ancient Greece could be used to highlight the political implications of Shakespeare's works, including *Hamlet*
- the birth of democracy could be used not only to deepen your understanding of the teachings of Plato and Socrates, but also to widen your grasp of the philosophy of John Stuart Mill
- the theory of the self from your Philosophy course could feed into your understanding of the development of the novel, with its depiction of the self, and the work of James Joyce and his interior monologue and stream of consciousness narrative techniques
- your work on ethical issues and the theory of the self may have a bearing on your understanding of the character Hamlet and his struggle with the ethical issues that he faces
- the works of John Stuart Mill could be useful prompts in your thinking about the development of the novel as a reflection of, or escape from, society
- the questions asked by Descartes about the nature of existence and a sense of self may be answered, if only partially, within the novels that you read or within your reading of *Hamlet*.

These are, of course, just a few examples of how some of your modules might impact beneficially upon others. Once you begin to look, you will find connections *everywhere*. This is one of the pleasures of studying as an undergraduate and, if you are able to make even a few connections, you will be streets ahead of most of your fellow students.

Making connections between texts involves a similar process. It simply requires you to avoiding assuming that a novel is just a novel, for example. It is also a historical document, perhaps a social commentary upon a time and perhaps also a philosophical treatise in disguise. It asks that you do not presume, just because you are studying a Social Science module on a Monday morning in one department, that it can have no bearing on the French Literature course that you attend on the Wednesday, or the Politics seminar that you join on the Friday. Making connections between modules and texts in a single subject might seem easier and more obvious, but they are overlooked surprisingly often. The same process can be used for these as in the example given above, the only difference being that the connections will be even easier to find and use in your essays and projects.

The connection of ideas is more subtle than the process of making connections between modules and texts, perhaps because the ideas are often your own, and sometimes they can be unfocused at first. If you find yourself struck by an idea in a lecture or seminar, but you are not sure why or how it connects to other areas of your studying, make a note of it and come back to it later. You may well find that you have had a brainwave. Often the idea has little to do with what the lecturer is trying to say, so by storing it away you can ignore it for the moment and come back to it at your leisure and work out why it rang a bell for you, and perhaps how you can use the idea in connection with other ideas that you have read about or are developing for yourself. When you come to look back at your notes, perhaps for revision or to work up an essay, you may well find that the little jottings in the margin are the most inspirational aspect of the notes, particularly as you become more confident in your subject.

The connection between ideologies can be the most difficult connection to make, often because each theory, concept or ideology is difficult to grasp in itself. You are so busy trying to work out what is being said that the impact of one theory upon others that you have learnt about can tend to get overlooked. Indeed, if you are enthusiastic enough to get a reading list before you begin your study, you will often be encouraged to read a general book on the theory of your subject and this is often enough to put you off altogether. The most effective way to tackle the 'big ideas' within undergraduate study, whether they are political ideologies, the theory of language, concepts within Sociology or the major teachings of Philosophy, is to refuse to let them daunt you. When you are faced with complex ideologies or dense theories, there are techniques that you can employ to help you to get to grips with them. Firstly, do not allow yourself to be flustered or intimidated. If you are having difficulties, so will most of the people around you. Secondly, ask questions, even if they seem too simple. Your tutors are there to teach you, so use them. Thirdly, allow yourself the time for it all to sink it. Some theories and concepts only become clear once you have had the chance to reflect upon them and put them into practice. You *do* have time to do this, even if it feels as if time is passing too rapidly. After all, if you were expected to be able to grasp it all in an instant, the undergraduate course would only be about six months long.

If you are still having difficulties, despite your best efforts, ask for examples of each theory in action, as this can often make it clearer than any quantity of lectures. Remember that you may already be employing a methodology or utilising a concept that you have left unnamed. Undergraduates are often surprised to find that they have been employing a recognised and defined approach to a subject, without knowing what to call it. So, when looking for examples so as to clarify your thoughts, do not forget to look at your own work. Lastly, recognise that every undergraduate will leave university with at least one concept unmastered, one theory that is still only vaguely grasped, one ideology that will always remain no more than words on a page. You are not alone, and if you really feel that you are not going to 'get it', then find out just how vital it is and, if it is possible to do without understanding it in its entirety, move on to the next stage of your studying.

Once you feel confident about the basic ideas contained within one particular theory or ideology, make very simple notes about it, perhaps just a few keywords on an index card that will serve to jog your memory in the future. It is often the case that something that is familiar in your first year has become as clear as mud by the third year and a few keywords can be invaluable. They can also help you to make connections. Every so often (not necessarily more than every few months) you can take a look through the cards and you will be pleased to find that the aspects of your subject that you have studied so far *are* connected, one ideology *can* inform another and all of this can be used to your advantage in managing your degree. The best way to approach this, as with so many other areas of your life at university, is to begin early. It is frustrating to begin to fill out index cards halfway through your course, realise that it is a good idea that will work for you and then to have to go back tediously through all your earlier course notes, wishing that you had begun earlier. Another aspect of university life that is best tackled as early as possible is the issue of assessment and it is to this that we will move now.

▶ Assessment procedures

The assessment procedures that a university employs are very unlikely to have been amongst the criteria that you used to decide between one university and another. Indeed, it would be unusual if you had any clear idea of how you were going to be assessed before you reached university and began your course. Nevertheless, managing your degree effectively is, in large part, a case of successfully managing the process of assessment. There is no point in spending three or four years in a flat panic, believing that everything you do might be open to assessment and might influence your degree result (and there are students who do feel like this for much of their course); neither is it a good idea just to ignore the question of assessment until it is too late to manage the process to your benefit. If you are clear about what is expected of you and when you are required to deliver, you will be in a better position to make the most of your time and effort. In Chapter 5 we will be looking at your degree profile options and considering the impact of different forms of assessment upon your decision-making. Here, I will be outlining the principal methods of undergraduate assessment and pointing out the essential points to remember in each area.

There are seven common ways by which your performance might be assessed: essays, seminar papers, presentations, coursework, dissertations, vivas and special projects. Your subject might also have additional specific requirements: you may be asked to give a public presentation; if you are studying a language, you will certainly be required to undertake a spoken examination; if you are studying music or the performing arts, there will be a performance element to your assessment. What is not usually directly assessed are less formal, practice essays, your general seminar performance or record of attendance. Of course, in extreme cases, it may be that a lack of attendance will jeopardise the right of a student to sit an examination or gain a degree, and it is inevitable that, because lecturers are only human, a brilliant performance in seminars during the term is likely to ensure that any written work you produce is approached with a favourable disposition. Having said that, no lecturer is going to mark you down on an essay just because you are quiet in seminars (unless you have been told that a seminar discussion will constitute part of the overall assessment). So, the message here is to spend your time learning what all the different assessment procedures involve and how to achieve well in them, rather than panicking about every little thing that you do.

Essays

Essays are probably the form of assessment with which you are most familiar. Even if you are a mature student who has not studied for some time, you will be amazed at how quickly it all comes back to you. There are plenty of study skills guides available to help you with producing essays (you will find some help on this subject in the recommended reading section at the end of this book). The focus here, in terms of the overall management of your degree, is how best to manage the production of the essays that will be required of you. There are three main points to remember. Firstly, ensure that you know exactly what is required of you in each essay. This may sound obvious, but one difference between your earlier work and undergraduate study is the nature of essay titles. You may well be given several title options for each essay, you may even be asked to make up a title for yourself, which will then be approved by your tutor. In some cases you will be expected to write about an area of your subject that receives little support in lectures and seminars, and on these occasions you will be expected to do some independent research. Whatever the situation, do not be afraid to ask the advice of your tutor. If you feel hesitant about this, talk to your fellow students in the first instance and assess their interpretation of a question, just to make sure that you are on the right track.

Once you have decided upon and fully understood the question, you will need to make sure that you are clear about the length of essay that is required of you. Most undergraduate essays tend to be about 1500–3000 words in length, but more extended essays may be required if they are intended as practice essays for later coursework, so make sure that you are clear about this. If a course is entirely assessed by coursework, it would not be unusual for you to be expected to produce several pieces of formal, assessed work of between 3000 and 8000 words. Although this can seem daunting, try not to let yourself be put off by word counts. Students often look aghast when they realise that they are expected to produce an essay of more than 5000 words, and yet most will realise, within a few weeks of the deadline, that this is not nearly enough for them to say all that they want to say. The third aspect of managing essay writing is to work out the timing and then plan according to how you work best. There is probably no point, if you have always been a last-minute person, in deciding that, now you are an undergraduate, you really will plan your work more methodically. You already have a way of working that has suited you in the past and will work for you in the future. One exception to this is if you are being continually assessed by your performance on a week-by-week basis and so cannot rely on a last-minute spurt of energy, but you are unlikely to take this sort of course if you know that this is not how you work best; we will be discussing this in more detail in later chapters.

Seminars

Seminars are the backbone of university teaching. They consist of groups of students (usually 10–20) meeting together, usually every week, under the guidance of a tutor in order to discuss aspects of their course. Sometimes the tutor will lead the discussion, sometimes students are asked to become more directly involved. Seminar papers and presentations cause a lot of consternation amongst undergraduates because they can feel so alien as a way of expressing yourself. If you are used to producing essays and maybe taking part in discussions within a classroom situation with a familiar group of people, it can be frightening to be asked to give a seminar paper in the third week of your first term. However, as with essays, there are certain generalisations that apply to seminars that can help you to cope. The first thing to bear in mind is that if you do not turn up for the seminar at which you are due to present a paper, you will leave your tutor (and perhaps your presentation partner) in the lurch and with little option but to fail you, so it is well worth letting your tutor know if you cannot make it. This is unlikely to be a major problem, as long as he or she is warned in advance. The second thing to consider is whether you are being asked to give a seminar paper or a seminar presentation: you should be given plenty of guidance on this. Essentially, a seminar paper is just as it sounds: you will write down what it is that you want to say, either in note form or as if it were an essay, and simply read it to your seminar group. These are often introduced as part of the learning process and are not normally marked as part of your undergraduate assessment. They are used as one way of getting a seminar group to work together and make sure that everyone in the group prepares well for at least one week of the term. A seminar presentation, on the other hand, may involve you being marked upon your presentation performance. With the increasing stress being laid upon the oral communication and presentation skills of undergraduates, this type of seminar is becoming more common and it is important that you know if this is what is expected of you, as up to 50 per cent of the marks available to you may be based upon your presentation skills.

There are, for the most part, two different types of seminar paper or presentation. You might be asked to introduce a topic, either by yourself, as one of a pair or part of a group. All that is required here is that you do the reading and then lay out the basic facts so that your seminar group (many of whom will not have read the relevant texts) can then discuss the topic in question. You would typically be asked to present for five or ten minutes in a one-hour seminar. This should not be a problem for you. A little nerve wracking, perhaps, the first time you do it, but you will not be expected to be an expert on the subject or engage in extended argument to support a point of view or a theory. Seminar papers or presentations such as this are unlikely to be marked as part of your course. The second type of seminar paper or presentation is one in which you are asked to take a topic and present a point of view. This is likely to involve a more extensive piece of work (you might be asked to talk for about 15 minutes) and may take the form of a more formal presentation. You will sometimes find that two students are asked to speak in one seminar, perhaps arguing from opposing viewpoints or tackling different aspects of an especially thorny subject. Within this context, you might be expected to answer some questions from the other members of the group or support your argument against their opposition.

Presentations

These are an increasingly popular form of assessing Humanities and Social Science undergraduates. Essays show that you can articulate an extended argument, seminars show that you can think on your feet and presentations show that you can present yourself, and your arguments, in a way that will stand you in good stead once you begin your career, and as such, they are useful opportunities for you as well as your tutors. As with essays, there are books available offering guidance on presenting, but here I will outline the points that you will need to bear in mind as you begin to prepare for your first presentation. Firstly, make sure that, if it is to be a team presentation, your team will work well together. This is easy if you are choosing your team, but if you are allocated team members and one of them is a weak presenter, be aware of this from early on and make sure that that team member is supported whilst being given the least possible opportunity to hamper the presentation. Secondly, be absolutely clear about what is expected of you in terms of the logistics of the presentation. Have you understood the presentation title completely? Are you to use visual aids? Is a handout to be produced? Will there be questions at the end? Who will be in the audience? Knowing all these things in advance will help you to feel more confident and avoid any nasty shocks on the day.

The most important thing to get right in terms of managing the presentation is timing. If this goes wrong, it will cancel out most of the good work that you have done. If a presentation is due to run for 15 minutes, nobody is likely to notice if it only runs for 14 minutes, but as soon as you hit 17 minutes, people will start to fidget and become anxious on your behalf, and by 19 minutes you will probably be asked to stop, regardless of whether you have finished. The secret is to aim to speak for a few minutes less than the time allotted to you, and you will then find that you are on time on the day. You will also need to be aware, at the outset, of how the presentation is to be marked. There is no need to become overly concerned about making everything perfect if the presentation performance is not being marked and only the content is being taken into account. Of course, you will want to do it as well as you can and make it look as good as possible, but you will focus your efforts in a far more effective way, concentrating your time where it is needed, once you know exactly how you are to be marked.

Coursework

Coursework can take various forms, but what is common to all coursework is that it will be assessed as part of your course as you develop rather than by examination. Making decisions about how well this might suit you will be explored in Chapter 5, but there are three points to be aware of in terms of the management of the assessment of coursework. Firstly, and most importantly, timing is crucial. There will always be a deadline and you will be penalised (usually quite heavily) if you miss it. On the positive side, you can usually expect to be well supported as you prepare the coursework, with plenty of access to your tutors and guidance as you go along. Lastly, you may have the opportunity to undertake research of your own, under the guidance of your tutor, so if you like working on your own or have an area of particular interest, coursework might be your best option.

Dissertations

Dissertations can be part of coursework assessment and they often occur as part of a degree in which two (or sometimes more) subjects are being studied. They are called by several different names, but they are all lengthy pieces of written work (typically 12,000–20,000 words) that are intended to represent an extended period of study. In order to manage your dissertation effectively, you will need to bear in mind several key points. Firstly, find out as early as you can exactly what is expected of you in terms of timing, word count and title, just as you would for an essay. Secondly, find out which lecturer will be supervising you in preparing the dissertation and, if it is a lecturer with whom you have difficulty, sort out the problem in the early stages. You may find that you get on much better once you are working in his or her area of interest and on a one-to-one basis, but if the lecturer is rarely available or has obviously taken a dislike to your methods of working, talk to your personal tutor to see what can be done to change your dissertation supervisor.

Although your department or departments will offer general guidance as to the dissertation length, timetable for submission and requirements in terms of presentation, never assume that this is all you need to know. Confirm with your supervisor (and the departmental secretary) that the information you have is the most up to date and is accurate and relevant to your particular dissertation. Once you are sure of the requirements, you can begin to plan, and getting this right is essential. Again, there are guides available for dissertation writing, but in general terms your plan should leave you enough time to think about the dissertation, research it, think about it again, write it, think about it yet again and then check it. This last task always takes longer than you ever thought possible, and is best done by you and someone else, as we always tend to read what we wanted to write rather than what we actually did write.

As you progress with your dissertation, take a look at other recent examples within your department. They are often kept by the administrative staff or tutors for future reference, and one glance at a complete and well-received dissertation can help to save you hours of poring over a style guide as to the laying out of the pages or the best way to produce the footnotes. You can also pick up good ideas from looking at the work of your predecessors, such as whether illustrations are common and the length of introductions and (crucially) bibliographies. The last aspect of managing your dissertation is to know when to get help. Things can go wrong, and even the most minor glitch can seem like an almighty disaster when you are three weeks from the deadline. As with so much else, the answer here is just to yell for help as soon as you know that things are not as they should be. Problems are usually solved quite easily. However awful it seems to you, your tutor should know exactly what to do to help you out of the difficulty. If your tutor is unavailable when you reach panic level, do not waste time worrying alone. Go straight to the secretary whom you find most helpful in your department. He or she will certainly have seen it all before and will know how to make sure that you get the help you need.

Vivas

A viva (the universally used, shortened version of *viva voce*) should not even be thought about until it is absolutely necessary. They are one of the myths of university life. Every family friend can tell you the story of their (or their friend's) horrific viva, and yet most undergraduates will never have to undergo a viva. Vivas are most commonly used as a way of deciding if a student who is on the borderline between two different classes should receive the higher grade. There are some courses where a viva is a necessary formality for every undergraduate at the end of the course, but this is rare and usually only takes place on very specialist courses with small numbers of students. What makes vivas such an ordeal is the students' perception of them. It is only natural to be concerned, but there is no need for you to spend the time after your examinations revising all over again in case you get a viva before your result is finalised. That is the time to relax. If you are called to take a viva, you can be fairly certain that there will be no more than three other people in the room, one of whom will probably be your tutor, and that they will understand your nerves and ask you as gently as possible to expand upon an answer you gave in an examination. At this point, you take a deep breath and just talk to them. They want you to do well, they want to help, so work with them to allow them put up your grade.

Special Projects

These are an increasingly common part of undergraduate life, as universities become more responsive to the needs of industry and student expectations of a flexible approach to degrees. The management of your degree will include your plans for any special project that you intend to undertake and you may know already what it is you will be doing; but if you like the idea of working outside the traditional field of undergraduate studying, it is worth knowing the variety of special projects that can exist so that you can be on the lookout for them. These projects typically include career placements (also called work or industrial placements) that can run from three weeks to a year, trips to study or work abroad, and independent research projects outside your own department or even outside the university. Working outside the university might include, for example, working in a school running a theatre workshop, or studying at another university on a specific, relevant research project for an agreed period.

You are likely to be a student who either loves or hates the idea of special projects such as these. If you look into it early enough and are keen to get involved, you can certainly make the most of the opportunities that are there for you. If you hate the idea of working outside the traditional format, reading this section will have made you aware of this and you can make your choices accordingly.

Whatever choices you make and however you are assessed, you will need to get to grips with the basics of undergraduate study as soon as you can. This book, and other study skills guides, can help you in your work, but nobody can actually do the studying for you. Self-reliance and self-discipline are the cornerstones of a successful undergraduate life and it is essential that you consciously try to develop these qualities as soon as you begin to study. Many of the skills that you need in order to stay ahead will, of course, be second nature to you by now, but in the next chapter we will be looking at how to maximise your learning opportunities and make the most of the help you are given as an undergraduate.

Spot guide

The key points to remember from this chapter:

- make sure that your course is the right one for you
- assess your strengths and weaknesses and learn how to improve your performance
- think as widely as possible in every learning situation
- make connections between modules, texts, ideas and theories
- tackle the 'big ideas' head on and master them
- know exactly how you will be assessed and make the most of the assessment procedures

3 Maximising your Learning Opportunities

Troubleshooting guide

Read this chapter for help in the following areas:

- if you are unsure of the difference between primary and secondary texts
- if you feel overwhelmed by the range or number of books you feel that you should read
- if you are unused to planning your time in relation to your studying
- if you find your reading lists difficult to manage
- if your reading lists seem far too long
- if your reading lists are too short, or lacking detail and guidance
- if you want to find out how to boost your reading lists and how to find and use your own sources
- if you find information technology confusing, or are unclear how to use it to your advantage
- if you find it daunting to approach lecturers whom you do not know well
- if you would like to do more academic networking, but are confused as to how to go about it
- if you would like to know more about 'virtual tutorials'
- if you would like to be more creative and successful in making searches on your computerised library catalogue
- if you can never find the books that are on your reading list
- if you would like to improve your reading skills and style
- if you feel that there are just too many books in your life at the moment

▶ How to study texts effectively

If you do little else during your time at university, it is essential that you read and understand the principal texts on your course, those that form the basis of each of your modules. This may sound simplistic: you might be thinking, 'of course I will read the principal texts, that is what I have come to university to do'. However, most graduates could tell you of the text that they fully intended to read throughout the duration of their course and never quite got around to opening. Sometimes the problem is simply one of identifying those texts that are essential. If you are studying English Literature or a language, the situation is quite simple. You will be expected to master a range of texts in a set amount of time. If you are studying Politics or Philosophy, things might not be so simple. You will still be asked to read principal texts, but these may be heavily supplemented by so many other important works that it can be difficult to see the wood for the trees.

The second problem students can face is in identifying the difference between primary and secondary texts, particularly when they come to refer to them in essays or need to produce bibliographies. Although, as with every aspect of studying, opinions can differ, a safe rule of thumb is to refer to any text as a primary text if it is an original work of literature, or a piece of written historical or statistical evidence. So, for example, a novel would be a primary text, as would a court record, even if both were produced in a facsimile version. A critical collection of essays discussing the novel would be a secondary text, as would a text analysing the court records. You may not always have to make this distinction clear in your work, but it can be confusing and rather intimidating, if lecturers refer to primary and secondary sources and you are unsure of which is which.

Let us return to the problem of reading all the principal texts that you are required to study and the ways in which this can go wrong. This is how it happens. You are faced with an enormous reading list, but the principal texts are clear. In an English Literature course, as I have said, this is simple: novels, plays and poetry will form the hub of your reading task. In Philosophy, to take another example, you may be asked to study two or three principal books per term and back these up with supporting texts. You begin to read and feel quite confident in the first few weeks. This feels like familiar territory, not so dissimilar from your previous experiences, except that, as the pressure increases, you begin to get behind. A novel might be discussed in one week only and then be discarded as the next piece of literature is approached, or you may be faced with a pile of sociological evidence to analyse and by the time you have finished, everyone seems to have moved on.

It would be easy, but inaccurate, to assume that those undergraduates who fail to keep up with the reading are lacking commitment to their course or not working hard enough. In fact, it is often the most committed and interested students who fall behind, and this is where the management of your programme of study comes in. It might be because you are so keen, and try to read all possible secondary texts as you go along, that you are having trouble. Even if you are less than enthusiastic about one aspect of your course, you might be asked to give a seminar presentation or produce a course essay that requires you to do some backup reading, and this can also blow you off course.

The first thing to do is to work out a plan which will ensure that you cannot get behind without at least being aware of the problem and being able to take steps to overcome it. Of course, a counsel of perfection would be to assume that you will read everything which is required of you, including all the recommended secondary reading, in every subject, every term. It is probably far better to assume that this is unlikely but that, with planning, you will be able to achieve what is required of you during the term, and then work on additional reading in your spare moments and during the vacations. Chapter 4 will focus on how to use your vacation time to best effect, but at this stage I will outline one way in which you could plan a term's reading. I will assume for the purposes of this example that you are studying English, History and Sociology in your second term at university. The English course involves mastering seven primary texts; the Sociology course is based upon three principal areas of study, relying upon six set texts; the History course covers two principal areas of study, each supported by three principal texts.

Week One: Read Sociology texts one and two
Assess requirements of the term (seminar papers and
presentations, term and assessed essays)
This is essentially your Sociology week, allowing you to focus upon that subject more than the others. You will not be burdened with too much work, so you will be able to spend some time finding out what will be expected of you and plan the term.

Week Two: English text one already read in the holidays – read English
text two with some supporting reading of secondary texts
so as to prepare for seminar
Prepare Sociology essay, including reading secondary texts
This is a week of preparation, for both a seminar and an essay. The essay is likely to require more secondary reading than the seminar, which could be prepared after reading the set text and possibly referring to one or two secondary texts. There will still be time to do additional work, but your focus will be on preparing and writing.

Week Three: **Sociology essay due in**
English seminar paper to be delivered
Complete Sociology essay
History text one already read in the holidays – read text two
Prepare material for History group presentation

This is your busiest week so far, with last-minute finishing touches to be added to the essay and seminar paper. Giving the paper might be a bit nerve wracking, but whilst you are in the mood for seminars, beginning to prepare for your History seminar presentation is a good idea. Reading the History text will seem like a little light relief, and will help to keep the balance between reading, writing and speaking.

Week Four: Read English text three
Read History text three
Read Sociology texts three and four
Rehearsals for History group presentation

This is a reading week. Some departments in some universities set aside reading weeks, during which lectures and seminars are kept to a minimum. This is your reward for all the work that you got through last week. As you have organised your term and most of your fellow students will not have done this, you may well be able to take control of the timing of the rehearsals for the History group presentation, which will be to your advantage.

Week Five: **History seminar group presentation**
Assess progress in History – any secondary reading necessary to make things clear?
Begin to prepare History assessed essay

This is your History week. Giving the presentation will be an important task, particularly if you are being marked on your presentation skills and are working in a group, necessitating several last-minute rehearsals. Taking time to assess a subject is also important. This is not time off, but instead a chance to look at what you have achieved and plan what you will do next.

Week Six: Complete History assessed essay
Read English text four
Read History text four
Read Sociology texts five and six

Another reading week, although this time it will be busier. You will be able to balance your time between reading and completing your History essay.

Week Seven: History assessed essay due in
English term essay due in

This could be a great week if you have got through everything so far. If the essays are complete and handed in early in the week, this will give you the time to enjoy other things (such as celebrating your achievement with friends) and the mental space to consider the last third of the term. If things have not quite gone according to plan, this is the ideal week in which to catch up before you face the race to the end of term.

Week Eight: Read English text five
Read History text five
Assess progress in Sociology – any secondary reading
necessary to make things clear?

Another reading week, but this time with space allowed for you to assess your progress in Sociology and plan for the next stage.

Week Nine: Read English text six
Assess progress in English – any secondary reading
necessary to make things clear?

This is your English week. All the production work (your essays and seminar papers) is done and so you will now have time to consider how to plan your holiday work.

Week Ten: Sociology seminar paper
Prepare Sociology seminar paper
Read English text seven and do secondary reading for text
three, ready for holiday practice essay and examinations
Read History text six
Plan your vacation work

The Sociology paper has not been prepared the week before on this occasion, but you have done the reading and can feel confident that the paper can be written with relative ease. This week could be busy, as you get ready for the Sociology seminar and plan for the holidays.

As you can see, this is a detailed plan, perhaps a more detailed plan than you are used to preparing for yourself. It may be that in the past you have only ever planned your time like this when examinations were looming, but the benefit of this method of managing your studying will become clear to you as soon as you begin to do it. You will find, of course, that the requirements of your course will be different from the details included above, but a scheme such as this will still cover your needs. You will notice that the example is laid out in weeks, rather than dates being given, and this is one of the first aspects of university life to get used to. You will be given the dead-line for an essay as 'week six', or be asked to prepare a seminar paper for 'week four'; this can be confusing if you are used to being given dates rather than everything being calculated in weeks. An academic diary can help to overcome this confusion, although it may be simpler just to put 'week one', 'week two' and so on at the top of each week in your diary to remind you of where you are.

When you come to do your detailed plan, there are a few guidelines to remember:

- Make sure that you give yourself a 'week off'. Not really a week in which to do nothing, but a week (such as week seven above) when you can take the time to reflect upon what you have learnt and reward yourself for all your hard work.
- When it comes to assessing your progress, be strict with yourself about setting time aside to do this. Check that your notes are in order, write out your index cards on the 'big ideas' that you have conquered, check back through the reading lists to see where you can find out more about your weaker areas of understanding, do practice examination questions to ascertain how well you might perform in the future.
- Make allowances for some overlap. In this example, weeks one, five, seven and nine have been left looser than the others so that you can fit in other tasks as they become necessary. A plan such as this is not intended to be immovable – it should be flexible enough to allow you to respond to events without feeling that you are losing control. It should be possible to adapt your plan realistically if you fall behind in one week.

In the last week of this plan I have suggested that you take time to plan for your vacation work, and I discuss this in more detail in Chapter 4. Vaca-tion planning is one of the keys to success in managing your degree, and although you may be working to get some cash in the vacation, you will find the pressure of undergraduate work far less stressful if your vacations are planned as well as you have planned your timetable for each term.

One of the pleasures of producing a plan such as this is that it will instantly make you feel in control of your studying, rather than feeling that you are simply being handed a confusing array of tasks without being sure how you will be able to fit them all in. This plan shows what you are likely to need to get done in the term in order to keep up; it does not, of course, exclude the possibility of you doing any amount of secondary reading or additional research as you go along. If you can do this as well, you will have the sat-isfaction of knowing that you are exceeding your expectations: a nice posi-tion to be in.

▶ Reading lists and how to use them to your advantage

Once you have made your plan for the term, you will feel organised. This is always a good thing, if you are aiming to manage your degree rather than just feeling as if you are being dragged through it. Next you need to tackle the reading lists. It is easy enough to tell yourself that you need to do some secondary reading in a particular subject during one week of the term, and then find yourself faced with a seemingly impenetrable reading list. The main thing to recognise about reading lists is that, in most subjects, they are not designed to be read in their entirety and that some secondary texts will require only a partial reading. There are two reasons why they are often so huge: firstly, it is assumed that a hoard of students will attack the library at the same time, so you are given plenty of options so as to maximise your chances of actually getting a book; secondly, it is hoped that you will want to study some areas in depth (perhaps for an essay), and so will need a more comprehensive list of secondary texts in those areas than in others.

The quality of the reading lists produced by different departments and different universities varies widely. Some are very useful, giving you guidance as to the relative value of the proffered texts for a variety of uses. Sometimes you are simply given a lengthy list of options, sometimes (believe it or not) reading lists are too scant, offering just a few secondary texts for guidance. Your first task is to face each reading list head on and get to grips with it. You will probably be given all your reading lists at the beginning of each course, or at the commencement of each term. Now is not necessarily the time to analyse them in detail, but it is worth spending a little time reading through each list in order to make an initial decision about how well you are likely to be able to cope with it, to make sure that enough texts are listed for an area of interest that you are already developing, and to ensure that you know what is essential and what is supportive reading. A review of the relevant reading lists will take place when you reach the 'assessment week' in your plan for each subject.

Once you have the list in front of you, go straight to the library and see what is available. It can sometimes be reassuring just to look at the books in question, to flick through them so as to work out what each text is offering. By planning in advance, you will be able to avoid the rush to get at the few essential books that everyone else wants to get hold of for a set essay. Next, decide what sort of text you need as backup for the areas that you are working on for each week of the term. This will, to some extent, depend upon the type of reading that you find most appealing. Some students prefer to read just one or two books that give an in-depth evaluation of a subject or its history; others prefer collections of essay, which allow them to read about a range of perspectives on their area of interest. It is usually best to try to combine the two. If a subject is well covered by lectures and seminars, or if you feel that you know a fair amount about it from earlier studying, collections of essays are a good place to start, whereas a more fundamental guide may be needed in other areas so as to give you a good start in your studying.

There will inevitably be some primary texts that you back up with no more than one secondary text (if that), perhaps if you do not intend to cover the subject as a preferred option in your examinations, or because you are just using it to enrich another area of interest. However, if you do intend to read several secondary texts, the reading lists are just a starting point. There are several ways in which you can personalise your reading lists:

- A book that you enjoy, written by an author whose writing you find easy to read and whose approach appeals to you, can offer you a lot more than simply the words that are contained within it. It is also likely to include a bibliography and/or a list of texts for recommended further reading, some of which might be by the same author. These will give you valuable clues as to where to go next, and will help you to stray, in a fairly safe way, from the reading list that you have been given.

- Similarly, indexes are handy places to linger when you are reading a recommended book or just browsing through the reading list. If you have an essay to work on or a seminar paper to prepare, you will have a specific area to explore and keywords looked up in indexes will lead you straight to that area in any book. You may not read the whole book or even the complete chapter on your subject; a trawl through the index might point you towards useful paragraphs, offering you facts that can underpin your work or opinions that might confirm or refine the argument that you are making. You might also find passing references within the work to the opinions of other writers whose work you need to study.

- Browsing through bibliographies is similar to browsing along the library shelves, with the exception that strolling along the shelves gives you instant access to the books that appeal to you. Serendipity is a wonderful thing: just happening across a book whose author entirely supports your argument or which gives you exactly those facts that you need for your essay. There are a couple of points to remember when you have a go at trying your luck with library serendipity. First, check the age of each book that appeals to you (the publishing details are on page iv and include the date of first publication). It may not matter if it is an older book if it is a key work on the subject, but if it is more than a few years old and not on your reading list, approach it with a little caution. Do not assume that what is contained within the book is necessarily the last word; more recent research may have overtaken it. If you have any doubts about a book, it is far better to check with your tutor than to rely upon it (however tempting this may be, if it supports your argument) and then find that it has been discredited by recent scholarship.

• The help that your tutor can give you goes beyond just checking whether a book that you have found by chance is worth citing extensively in your essay. Lecturers have specialist areas of interest and know of many valuable books that have not made it onto the reading list, usually because of lack of space. If you are not sure which lecturer to ask about additional reading, it is worth checking the names of a few of your lecturers on your library's computerised catalogue (a handy thing to do anyway) to see who has written about the area in which you are working. If you approach a lecturer with a vague request for additional help, you are likely to be referred back to the reading list, but if you have a specific question about an area of study, or an essay title on which you are writing, you will probably find that the lecturer will be only too pleased to give the details of some additional books that are informing current debate.

• Your fellow students are also good sources of information. If they too have been spending time in the library chasing the books on the reading list, they will be able to give you their opinions of what is on offer: your academic networking begins here. Of course, their criteria for what is useful in a book may differ from yours, but if you talk with them about the books you will, at the very least, get an idea of what is contained within that mythical book that is on everybody's reading list and yet which has only ever once been found in the library. That way you will know whether it is worth your while to place a reservation for it and wait to read it before you complete your essay. Do not be put off placing a reservation for a book just because the library computer system assures you that it is not due back on the shelves for six weeks. In reality it is more likely to be returned within a few days, so place the order regardless of the due return date and then move on to find other books that could be of use to you.

The last thing to bear in mind as you work through a reading list is that you need to have confidence in your own ability to read. For all of us, there are writers whom we find easy and others whose style of writing is never going to be congenial to our way of taking in information. There will be areas of your subject that are inherently complicated and can never be transformed into an 'easy read', and facing that challenge is one of the pleasures of studying as an undergraduate. However, we all have experience of writers whose work we approach with enthusiasm, only to find that we are rereading each sentence two or three times and that we have lost the thread of the argument by the end of each paragraph. When this happens to you, you need to make a judgement on the situation. If the book is one of several secondary texts that are available to you, there is no need to feel that wading through the text is somehow a test of your intelligence, or that completing it is essential to you obtaining a good grade in your essay or seminar paper. Take a break from it and if you are still unable to get to grips with it by the next day, put it firmly back on the library shelf and move on to the next book. Managing your degree is largely about managing your time effectively, and wading hopelessly through what is, for you, a dense and almost incomprehensible text is not a sensible way to manage your time, neither is it good for your self-confidence.

► Using your own initiative

Reading lists will take you a long way towards where you need to be in terms of mastering your subject. Lectures, seminars and tutorials, in which you get the opportunity to discuss your own work, will get you the rest of the way in most cases. However, there are many other sources of information that can be of use to you and may not be available to, or considered by, your fellow students. These sources can give you a head start and also ensure that your work remains interesting and original in its approach to each subject:

- The first (and most often overlooked) source that is unique to you are your earlier courses of study. In your enthusiasm to move towards life as an undergraduate, you may be ignoring a vital resource. I have already mentioned the need to remember ways of studying that have served you well in the past, but your notes can also help to remind you of the fundamentals of an area of study that you have not visited for some time. Pre-university reading lists are often full of fairly basic texts, as well as more sophisticated works of scholarship, some of which you may never have read, and there is no shame in going back to baseline texts in order to get to grips with a new area, or to remind yourself of what you already know.
- Underutilised sources of library information are those shelves that house the journals and periodicals that deal with each subject area. These valuable resources can sometimes seem to be the best kept secret in university libraries and resource centres. Some students spend the first year or so at university without having any idea that such journals exist, as they are not always included on reading lists. You might overlook them because they are held on a different floor from your subject area floor,

so they are not right in front of you at every reading opportunity. Some collections are poorly catalogued, and so take time to explore, but such journals usually represent the cutting edge in research in your field, in manageable articles, and as such are invaluable to you, particularly as you may be one of the few students who will be quoting from these articles in your essays. It is not always made clear exactly what is available to you, even if you access your library's computerised catalogue, so spending time just browsing along the periodical shelves is well worth the effort, particularly as you can be fairly sure that other students will be too busy desperately trying to find the books on the reading lists to bother you much.

- Lectures can also inadvertently provide an insight into what you might read. As you sit in a lecture, you might find that the lecturer will discuss the views of a particular scholar, yet that writer's work might not be included on your reading list, either because his or her book has yet to be published, or because his or her work on the subject is confined to articles. As you listen to the lecture, make a note of any expert that is mentioned, including whether the lecturer is agreeing or disagreeing with the writer, and why, and then add that writer's name to your reading list. By the time you come to do the reading for a piece of work of your own, you will have a far more individualised list than your fellow students.

- Access to books is not restricted to your university library. Many departments hold collections of essays and articles and essential works of reference, and these are often housed in departmental reading rooms or other resource centres to which students have access, but which they rarely visit unless encouraged to do so. If you make a point of finding this resource room in your first term, you can then enjoy the sight of your fellow students dashing off to the library at the end of lectures, whilst you can just stroll down the corridor and study the same books with none of the hassle. Another advantage of departmental collections is their immediacy. As soon as a lecturer reads an article of interest, it can be copied and lodged with the collection, but you may not find out about it unless you happen to have the lecturer in question as your seminar tutor. By making regular visits to the resource room in your department, you will keep up to date with what is available, and the room itself is often a pleasant and quiet place to study.

- Once you have visited your own department's resource room, you are ready to start snooping around elsewhere. Social Science undergraduates, for example, might benefit from the specialised resources available in the History department, whilst students of French Literature might find valuable texts and articles in the English department library. You are unlikely to need written permission to explore the resources of any department, and, although you cannot usually remove texts from these resource rooms, an hour or so spent in them can save you a lot of time in the main library. Similarly, although you are unable to remove texts from special collections in the main library, it is worth finding out what is held in them. These collections are often held in a designated area of your library, guarded by archivists, and typically include Early Modern texts, valuable music collections and manuscript material, both Modern and Early Modern. If you think that this material could be of use to you, your tutor will be able to arrange for you to spend some time analysing it.

- In Chapter 2, I stressed the need for you to think as widely as possible about each topic that you study, and to use every resource available to you, and the point is worth repeating here. Newspaper and magazine articles are often produced by academics and can be worth following up. Television programmes can also provide useful reinforcement to your study. More specialist television and radio programmes are an easily accessible resource. Broadcast listings magazines will give you details of the Open University schedule of programmes, for example. By watching these programmes, you might discover a new approach to a problem or simply reinforce what you know already – a useful way of revising without you even realising it. There is a further benefit to watching such programmes. You will be spending much of your time at university reading books and articles, listening to lectures or discussing your ideas in seminars. Watching a TV programme cannot replace these activities, but it will provide a different way of taking in data, and this tends to boost your uptake of the available information.

- One resource available to you, especially if you are a mature student, will be indirect and may not be obvious to you at first glance. If you have had a career that is relevant to the subject you are now studying, you may find that some of your academic work is simply formalising and reinforcing your own experience. Try not to assume that, because you are at university, you have to confine yourself to the texts that are before you. If you have relevant 'real-life' examples to give in order to reinforce your arguments, do not be afraid to use them. Although you will have to avoid relying too heavily upon hearsay to the detriment of academic analysis, as supporting evidence your own experiences can enliven and sharpen the points that you want to make. As with all areas of your undergraduate life, nothing need be wasted and a multiplicity of resources can be utilised in order to further your understanding of your subject. This includes the use of information technology, to which we will turn next.

▶ Information technology

Whenever the term 'information technology' is used in relation to studying, the Internet springs to mind and it can be a useful tool, but one that must be managed carefully. You will probably be entirely familiar with the Internet and be happy to use it within your programme of study, but it is a bit like going on a shopping trip for information. Like any shopping trip, if you know what you want and where to get it, and you stick rigidly to your shopping list, you will have an efficient trip, hopefully returning home with the items that you need at a reasonable price. If you just wander aimlessly around the shops, you will return with nothing, or with several overpriced items that you had no idea that you wanted (and almost certainly do not need). When using the Internet, having no clear idea of where you are going can lead you to spend far too much of your valuable time searching fruitlessly for inspiration, being lead astray onto a dozen sites that are not really going to help you and finding that you are running out of time to read the books that you need to study, or to actually write your essay or prepare for your seminar.

So, be wary of how you spend your time and try to find out in advance where the information that you need is likely to be. Having sounded that note of caution, the Internet is an extremely useful place if you know where you are going, and undergraduates often fail to realise that several academic journals are available on the Internet, as are details of many conferences. If you have seen a conference advertised that is of interest to you, but you feel hesitant about attending, maybe because you are broke and it is being held 200 miles from your university, find out whether the papers are to be made available on the Internet. These are called the proceedings of a conference and, although it can sometimes take a little time for them to appear on the Internet, you will be able in this way to get some of the benefits of the conference or seminar without actually having been there.

One other word of caution about the Internet: it is not worth giving in to the temptation to buy essays on the Internet, however impressive they may seem. This is a booming industry just at the moment, and most of us have heard the stories of students buying whole essays and passing them off as their own, or being a little more canny and adapting the essays with little real thought about what they are doing or the quality of what they are producing. The problem with this scam, apart from the fact that you will come unstuck in examinations, is that university lecturers really do spend idle moments looking at these essays for themselves, particularly those within their subject area. Plagiarism (passing off somebody else's comments or research as your own) is one of the worst infringements of university regulations and will always be taken seriously and punished severely. A fake is easy to spot, so the odds on getting caught out are extremely high, not to mention the fact that, by regurgitating a pre-existing essay, you are learning nothing and, in the end, will achieve nothing.

The information technology resources available in your university library or resource centre will probably be the first source of data with which you will become familiar. Most university libraries run extensive education programmes aimed at all undergraduates, including tours and instruction sessions in the use of computerised catalogues. They may also run 'drop-in sessions', which allow you to check up on any aspect of IT at university about which you are unsure. If you miss out on the initial tours (and this is easy to do, as they are often run in your first week or so at university, when your attention is being pulled in all directions), make sure that you catch up with the tour at some time during the first term, as they are fairly brief and the librarians work hard to make them interesting and relevant to all the students. What may not be included in your guided tour are details of the CD-ROM information held in the library. These CDs are usually kept behind the library desks and are only available upon request and sometimes under a level of supervision. The existence of CDs which catalogue the books and articles in your area of study may become apparent to you as you progress, although they can present some of the same dangers as the Internet, as you wade through a seemingly endless number of books. They are especially useful, however, for finding essays and books by writers who have been mentioned in passing in lectures but whose work is not held in your library. Once you have their details, you can access your university's interlibrary loan system (another well-kept secret) and order them. What may never become apparent to most undergraduates is that your library will probably also hold CDs containing catalogues from other libraries (such as the British Library or the Bodleian Library) and CDs of dictionaries, newspaper archives and other valuable material that you may have trouble accessing in any other way. By just asking the librarians to give you a list of the CDs that are available, you could save yourself time and boost your resources base.

If you need some guidance in mastering the use of a CD-ROM or the Internet, and your library cannot help, find out how active your IT services department is. These departments (which go under several different titles) are often excellent sources of help and support, running a vast range of courses which are available to all students. Although you may not have any great interest in IT for its own sake, university is a great place to gain skills in areas of IT that you might need in the future. If you take these courses now (and they are often no more than a few hours long), you will find that you have an impressive portfolio of IT skills to offer to an employer later on, and the best thing about them is that they are usually free.

As a more direct part of your studying, your IT services department will be able to help you to keep up with developments in virtual tutorials and emailing. Virtual tutorials on the Internet are growing rapidly in popularity, and some courses at university (typically those that require little interactivity beyond that which can be achieved on the Internet) are taught predominantly via the Internet. Career development modules, for example, are taught with increasing enthusiasm within universities, and much of the work that you are required to do on these modules, such as producing a CV, researching a variety of careers or undertaking self-analysis in terms of your career choices, can be done effectively via the Internet. The move towards virtual teaching is not restricted to generic subjects such as this, and a mastery of the techniques involved in virtual tutorials is becoming increasingly important. The technological requirements placed upon students in these situations are kept to a minimum, but if you are not an IT enthusiast, support from IT services, your library or department will allow you to make the most of what is available, so do not hesitate to voice any concerns that you have: support and guidance is there for the taking.

In addition to formalised systems of information gathering and learning on the Internet, less formal communication between tutors and tutees via email is increasingly common. This way of communicating has an advantage for tutors, in that they can 'talk' to their tutees at a time that is convenient for them, having given some thought to the query that has been raised. It can also have enormous advantages for you. If you are shy about approaching a lecturer, perhaps because you have never seen him or her outside the lecture theatre, then email can be the best way to make a succinct enquiry about a subject and get an answer that is useful to you, without having to wait about nervously in the corridor hoping that you will bump into the lecturer as he or she comes past. Email communication can also help if you have a query that you are finding difficult to articulate. If what is really worrying you is that you do not understand a primary sociological theory, for example, you might sit in a seminar and ask questions which vaguely relate to the theory, hoping that the tutor will be inspired to outline the whole theory in words that you will understand, rather than having to admit outright that you do not understand what it is all about. You will still use the books available to you as your first point of reference but, if it still remains unclear, it is often easier to email your query, perhaps asking for a more specific reference to an essay or article that deals exclusively with the theory, than to face the tutor directly.

Hopefully, in a case such as this, the lecturer will point you towards the necessary book and also ask whether you would like to meet up to talk about the problem, and this gives you the advantage of going to a meeting where you are both clear as to why you are there. This is also true of lecturers who have not taught you for several terms. What might have seemed clear to you in your first term can become surprisingly fuzzy by your third year, and this can be quite alarming, particularly if you only realise that there is a problem as you approach an examination. You might feel diffident about approaching a lecturer who you suspect may not remember you, or who you feel may become impatient with you for needing further explanations so long after the event. In fact, lecturers are quite used to this and will be pleased to see that you are taking their lecture so seriously as to come back to it and tackle the issues afresh in your third year, but emailing a lecturer under these circumstances, at least as an initial method of contact, can be an appealing option.

It is always worth finding out, if you can, whether your lecturers in different subjects are keen on emails and IT generally. Some tutors love to receive essays on disk and will happily communicate with all their students via email. This is great if you too like emailing, and can lead to constructive relationships via email that save you the problem of trying to find a tutor and hoping to catch him or her at just the right time. However, there are a few lecturers (as there are some students) who will never feel comfortable with this means of communication, and therefore rarely open their emails, and will give only the most cursory answers to email queries. The good news here is that, if you know about this (by simply asking a lecturer if he or she prefers to be contacted via email or in person), you can avoid the problem. You will probably find that the lecturer who loathes emails is perfectly happy to see students in person and so there will, in fact, be no real problem.

Email communication with academics can be extended beyond your university. If you attend a conference or have a visiting speaker in whose work you are interested, collecting an email address for future reference allows you to access their knowledge and experience at any point in your course. If you have also given them your email address, you might find yourself on some useful email address lists, and in this way you can keep up with events that are being organised in your field. Similarly, within the university, if you have attended a seminar in a department in which you are not studying regularly, or if you have to work with students whom you rarely see, email is the ideal way to keep up connections without having to spend time arranging meetings or attending further events.

I have already suggested that joining the guided tours of the library can save you hours of fruitless searching time when you are in a hurry towards the end of your first term, but there are times when hours (well, perhaps minutes rather than hours) of potentially fruitless searching can be a good thing. Once you have been given an essay title, you will usually need to boost your reading list (either because you are really keen or because the books that you need have all disappeared from the library shelves) and so you will probably decide to type a keyword from the title of the essay into the library catalogue system and see what it offers you. Incidentally, most students, finding that several books on the reading list are out, overlook the possibility of typing in the names of the authors, as they may have written several books on a subject that might be relevant. So, you have typed in a keyword and the computer does its work. The temptation is to pick out just those books that are clearly the most relevant to the topic and leave behind those with less obvious titles. This is fine if you are in a hurry and have no need to read extensively, but if you do have a little more time, give the computer system a chance. If it is offering you a book, it could be because the content details entered into the system for that book include the keyword that you have typed in, or you might have been lucky enough to find a book that deals with a similar subject within a different context.

Let us say, for example, that you have been asked to look at the historical progress of the Cold War during the mid-1940s and early 1950s. You type in 'Cold War' as your search term and the system offers you a variety of texts. A text entitled *The History of the Cold War* will be an obvious choice, as would a book entitled *The Causes of the Cold War*. However, writing an essay about the history of the Cold War will require you to understand something of the political theories dealing with events at that time, so you may also choose to check out a book with the less obvious title *Cold War, Hot Politics*, even though this may be in a different section of the library to the one that you usually visit. Having done all of this, you can 'waste' a bit of time just browsing through what you are being offered. A book with the title *One Small World* may seem to be entirely irrelevant, until you realise that the search for 'Cold War' has selected this book because, in its brief catalogue synopsis, it has been noted that it deals with the political aftermath of the Cold War. Equally, a book entitled *Bold Moves* may be dealing with the activities of one political figure for just a few years in the 1940s. A book as specialised as this will not necessarily help with your overview of the subject, but it may help to support your argument with an apt and interesting illustration, an example that nobody else will have discovered. Of course, the rules that I mentioned for serendipity in the library still apply. You have to ensure that the books that you use are recent enough to be an accurate reflection of current thinking in your field, and that they have not been discredited for some reason. With that proviso in place, this example shows how, by spending perhaps 20 extra minutes in the library, you can significantly enhance your work, produce interesting material and save yourself time and the frustration of waiting for books that will not be available in time to be of any great use to you.

Of course, 'Cold War' is not the only search term that you could use. Be creative about your searching, and try typing in search terms that are rather less obvious, in this case perhaps the name of a politician about whom you have learnt, or the name of a town or country in which significant events occurred. When you are faced with a pile of books, some of which will be less relevant or useful to you than others, you will have no need to read through each book in its entirety. Managing your reading techniques will be a key feature of managing your degree, as the next section will reveal.

▶ How to read: a guide for the undergraduate

You might be tempted to skip this section, reasoning that of course you know how to read, given that you are already at university. However, you will be surprised at how many demands will be made upon your differing reading skills whilst you are an undergraduate. You will already know about your preferred style of reading (slow and steady, fast and furious, patchy but productive), but life as an undergraduate demands that you learn to skim read effectively, work steadily through set texts and read at speed whilst taking notes when the pressure is on. Taking notes is a skill that you will already have developed in your earlier studying, but it is worth mentioning here that the notes that you take, whether from lectures, seminars, books or the Internet, must show clearly the distinction between your ideas and those taken from elsewhere. As I have already mentioned, plagiarism is a risk that is simply not worth taking, and most students would be indignant at the very suggestion that they would do such a thing, but you can find yourself quoting another source entirely by mistake if you are not very careful to make your sources clear in every set of notes that you make. If you get into the habit of marking and naming your sources at every stage, you will protect yourself from this risk and the results of plagiarism, which are always severe within the academic community.

There are books available to help you to expand your range of reading skills, but the key to managing your reading during your degree is to recognise that, at any one time, you are likely to have up to five different sorts of books to hand, each sort making different demands upon your skills:

1. You will have *set texts* with which you will become familiar over the course of your study. The secret with these is not to let them overwhelm you. You will have to read several set texts in the first few weeks of your degree, and this should be done with some care, but you need not force yourself to understand every paragraph, or pressurise yourself to grasp every concept in its entirety. These books will be revisited during the course of your degree, so you will be reading knowing that you will be tackling them in depth in manageable chunks as the course progresses and your understanding increases.
2. You will have essential *backup reading* to do in order to support the set

texts, lectures, seminars and the work that you are producing. These are often available on limited loan time in the library and you may find yourself returning to them again and again. These are books that you may want to buy, so as to save yourself the frustration of not being able to get hold of them at crucial moments, but the reading skills involved in using them will be different from those demanded by the principal, set texts. You will be approaching these books with your lecture, essay and seminar requirements in mind, and with an awareness of what is contained within your set texts. You are much more likely, therefore, as you make notes on these books, to be arguing with some of the premises contained within them and comparing theories. This reading is much more active in many ways. You are not expected to soak up the book in its entirety, but rather to use it as an aid to sharpen your reasoning skills and deepen your understanding.

3. You will be using some books as an *immediate aid* in producing a specific piece of work. These books are often (and sometimes most usefully) collections of essays, and you may well need the book in order to read only one or two of the essays in the collection. You are unlikely to read these books from cover to cover, and you will be skim reading many of them; you might simply browse through the index to find the one or two references within the text that may be of use to you. These are also the books from which you are most likely to be photocopying sections or even single pages. It is far easier to attach a photocopied section to your own notes than to make extensive notes of your own, but there are two points to remember whilst you do this. Firstly, make sure that you make an exact and extensive note of the title, author and publication details of the book on your photocopy. There is nothing more frustrating than having to waste valuable time in the library trying to hunt out a book to which you wish to refer, but the details of which you forgot to take at the time. It can also be disastrous, if you have photocopied a section of a book that is now out on loan for three months, or that only came to you in the first place via the interlibrary loan system.

You also need to make sure that you take ownership of the information contained within the photocopied section or chapter. It is a lovely feeling to have spent the morning in the library, photocopying all sorts of useful information, and then to put all the photocopies neatly into plastics wallets in your files. Sadly, you may then ignore them for weeks or even months and then realise that you have no idea, when you come to look at them, why you ever thought that they were relevant, or to find that, because you have not highlighted the relevant sentences, you have to struggle through vast tracts of material before finding the one reference that you need. So, you must decide in advance to divide your time equally between identifying and finding the books, photocopying the relevant sections and then highlighting the sections or sentences that you will need for future reference. Then you can put them in plastic wallets in your files and feel truly virtuous.

4. You will have books that you have set aside for *leisure reading*. These will include the latest thrillers or romantic novels, as well as books dealing with issues on the periphery of your course, texts which you will probably not have to make notes on, but which will be useful in terms of giving you background information. If, for example, one of your modules is in American Studies, reading a selection of novels by American authors will be both enjoyable and useful. However, you will need to balance this leisure reading. If you know that you are the sort of reader who can never relax and so make notes on the American novel that is meant to be for leisure reading, or if you find that you sleep badly if you read anything related to your course, then finish off with a good trashy novel each night, or allow yourself occasionally to read something in your leisure time that is entirely unrelated to your field.

5. The last set of books that might haunt your undergraduate days are those which you feel that you *ought to read*, even though they are too dense to get to grips with, or too simplistic to hold your interest. These will tend to gravitate towards the bottom of the pile, and the management technique to employ here is to make yourself have a good clear out of your book pile at the end of each term. If a book has been sitting, unread, on the pile, be honest with yourself. Are you ever going to read it? Is it essential to your course? Is it enhancing your undergraduate experience? If the answer to all these questions is no (and it probably will be), be ruthless with yourself and return the book to the library. It will be available later if you suddenly need it, but at least it will not be in your sight all the time.

Once you have grasped that the huge pile of books loitering meaningfully in the corner of your room, or relentlessly weighing down your bags, can in fact be divided into these five categories, you will feel far more in control. You know that some of the books will be read in their entirety over the course of a few weeks or months, but you also have the consolation of knowing that most of them will be read only partially, and in a very different style from the way in which you will approach the set texts. Books viewed in this way become tools to be used in a variety of ways, not all of which are too time consuming. You will be able to use your differing reading skills to plan your reading schedule according to your mood, work commitments and energy levels, and to get on constructively with one of the most enjoyable activities of university life: reading.

Spot guide

The key points to remember from this chapter:

- read and understand the principal, set texts of your course
- tackle your reading lists head on and make them work for you
- customise your reading lists
- plan each term's work in detail
- be creative in your searching on the library's catalogue system
- find and use your department's resource room
- use books for their content, but also for their indexes and bibliographies
- find and use your own, unique sources
- get help with information technology if you need it
- use the Internet with caution
- find your library's CD-ROM collection
- vary your reading style to suit both the book you are reading and the work you are doing

4 Making the Most of your Time

Troubleshooting guide

Read this chapter for help in the following areas:

- managing the first six weeks of your course
- settling in to your hall of residence
- making the most of Freshers' Fair
- getting your bearings on the main university campus
- if you are not sure where to go for help in the first few weeks at university
- if you are confused about registering with the library and in your department, or as a member of the National Union of Students (NUS)
- if you hate filling out forms and tend to ignore them
- if you need help with using information technology
- if you have any sort of special educational need
- if English is not your first language
- if you are a mature student, concerned about fitting into university life
- if you have problems with your finances
- if you are not sure how to manage your vacation time to best effect
- if you are lacking balance between your work and leisure time; you always seem to get behind in your studying
- if you want to fit as much as possible into your time at university
- if you are not sure how to network effectively
- if you are concerned that you are saying too much or too little in seminars
- if you are unclear as to whether to make connections between your past experience and current studying

▶ **Managing your first six weeks as an undergraduate**

The first six weeks at university will be a challenge, particularly if this is the first time you have lived away from home. As well as coming to terms with this change, you will be faced with having to make many decisions, but there is a way through the maze, and this chapter will help you to settle into your new life as easily and productively as possible. As a new undergraduate, you will probably begin your first university term a week before the rest of the students; this is usually called 'freshers' week'. This early start is intended to help you to familiarise yourself with the university campus, meet your fellow students and sort out the administrative details of your degree before the hustle and bustle of the term proper begins. For some new undergraduates, though, this comes as a surprise; you are expecting to join a busy university campus but instead find a place that looks fairly deserted, almost eerily quiet in places. This can be disconcerting, but is a good time to get your bearings, in many different ways.

The university campus itself is unlikely to be a shock. You have probably visited it on an open day or at some point in the months leading up to the beginning of the new academic year. Most first-year students will have chosen a hall of residence. The first thing to do is to work out just what there is for you in the hall of residence. If you were able to choose it, you will already be aware of what is available in terms of the living accommodation and general facilities, but now you have to discover all the other things that will affect your first year at university. For some students, their first few terms will be spent in rented accommodation away from the campus, if their university has insufficient space to house them, but they will still be affiliated to a hall of residence. For them, it is even more important to make the most of this connection to a hall of residence. The place to start is the notice board: see what social events have been arranged in recent months, if there is a lost and found section or cards displaying items for sale. It should also tell you who is on the student committee that helps to run the hall and what they do. Is there a welfare officer for the hall? Is there a social committee? Does the hall run its own social or charity events? Are they campaigning for better facilities? Lastly, and most importantly, do you feel that you might like to get involved? This last question is an important one because, over the next few weeks, you are going to be asked to join all sorts of societies and clubs, and it is easy to get carried away on the main campus and ignore the fact that your hall is going to be your home over the next year (at least) and you might like to get involved in making it as good a place to live as possible.

Next you need to work out the connections between your hall and the university itself. All universities differ in this respect; some maintain strong links between halls and campus, whilst in others the halls tend to be little more than places to sleep, with the life of the university centred firmly on the main campus. This depends to some extent upon the way things are arranged geographically. Universities with large campuses may have all their halls within the grounds, whereas universities set in the middle of towns or cities may have small halls scattered around the town and rather more cut off from the main campus. Whatever the situation in your university, you will need to check out the best way to get from your hall to your classes, which may be held in several different locations. Although the university brochure will have told you about public transport, find out if it is practical to walk or cycle, or if there is a university bus service that includes your hall (this is not usually mentioned in university brochures). This may all seem obvious, but it is frustrating to find that you are walking a long distance each day to get to a bus stop, only to find, in week five, that you could have saved yourself a lot of time and trouble. You might also like to think in advance about your transport home for the vacations. A card on the notice board in your hall might help you to find somebody else who is driving back to your area at the end of term and who would be happy to give you a lift and share petrol money, saving you a long train or coach trip.

The connections between halls of residence and the main university campus are more than geographic. You also need to find out what mix of students are in your hall. Universities differ in their approach to this: you may find yourself with other students in your faculty, school or department in your section of the hall, or you might be part of a completely random mix. It is useful to discover as early as you can whether anyone taking your course or courses is a near neighbour. You might not become great friends, but you will almost certainly find each other to be useful contacts. If you get hit with a virus in the third week of term, it will be handy to have somebody close by who can take notes for you, or let your tutor know what is going on. In some ways, contacts such as these can be more useful than friends when it comes to managing your degree. Although your friends are only a mobile phone call away, there is no guarantee that they will remember to make copy notes for you, or tell your tutor that you will be absent from an important seminar or tutorial. Your friends may be very helpful, of course, but if you find that a friend is a useless note-taker, you are faced with the awkwardness of feeling obliged to accept notes that will be of little help to you. Sometimes making arrangements with somebody whom you know less well is better: he or she will make a greater effort, knowing you less well, and realising that you will return the favour one day. So, try to spot someone in your hall who is taking some of the same courses as you and who seems like he or she might work hard, and then make the connection now, before you get hit by a virus and really need it.

The main university campus is the next place to explore. Some of the work will be done for you, if there are guided tours of the campus or your department, but it is more likely that you will explore your department as you go along, by registering with your tutor and departmental secretary and then attending lectures and seminars. Lectures might be held outside your department, though, so a stroll around your faculty or school building is a good idea. That way, you can spot where the coffee rooms are (sometimes called junior common rooms) and work out how to get to the main lecture theatres. Hopefully you will also find the less obvious facilities, such as your department's resource room or specialist library and any student computer rooms. These are useful finds; undergraduates frequently overlook them and queue for ages in the library trying to gain access to a computer, unaware that there are computers available somewhere in their own building. There may be other facilities in your building that you will need at some point in the term (and you may not be told about these), such as a photocopying room or an Internet access facility; if you know of their existence now, it will save you time when you need them in a hurry later.

As soon as you can, you need to find the departmental secretary's office. This is vital. You will soon find that he or she is the fount of all wisdom where your course is concerned. It is here that you will register for courses, find out about your options and keep up with the paperwork attached to your degree. It is also here, you will discover, where you end up if things go wrong. For example, the departmental secretary can tell you how to go about changing one of your options, whether a course is full and how you can leave university early one term to go on a family holiday without falling foul of the regulations. Departmental secretaries often seem able to wave magic wands and make all sorts of things happen with no problem at all, so it is worth finding out which secretary or secretaries are responsible for you (there may be several in your department, but not all of them will be involved with the undergraduate courses), and always make sure that you have filled out every form that they ask for, on time and legibly. Departmental secretaries have long memories. If all they know about you is that you took six weeks too long to fill out a form and send it back in your first year, you can be sure that they will recognise you when you come to seek their help over your third-year options.

Having found out what is available in your department, take the time to walk around the campus and familiarise yourself with what is there. This is never a waste of time. You will find the library, of course, and the location of the Students' Union is usually fairly obvious, but you can also pick up other useful information. If you like to work alone and in peace, you will want to find out where any student study rooms are situated, or if there are places in the grounds where you might go to work undisturbed. There is likely to be a student services office of some sort, where you might in the future be able to get help producing overheads for a presentation or learning how to manage a tricky piece of equipment. IT services is a good place to locate, particularly if they have a notice board about IT training sessions (these are often posted on the library notice board as well). Booking up for one of the first training sessions of the term will ensure that you get a place (these courses are often oversubscribed by the middle of term) and meet people who are not on your course and who might have handy information about aspects of life at your university. You will find the main campus canteen on your first day, but there are likely to be other places to eat and meet people and you will find these as you stroll around. You might also find your university market, usually held each week in your Students' Union and a good place to meet friends and find cheap books and other essentials.

Although universities do not always make this clear, your first week as an undergraduate is the best time to get as much of the administration out of the way as you can. Getting your library card on day one may seem a bit keen, but by day three the queue will be horrendous. Get four passport-sized photos as soon as you can: you will need them for your library and NUS cards (these serve a multitude of functions, not least of which is the discounts that you can get on all sorts of things) and your departmental registration. One photo booth between all the registering undergraduates makes for long queues by the end of the first week, when everyone realises that they need the photos before they can get anywhere. If you need any help from the Students' Union, try to get it now. They can provide help if English is not your first language, they can help you with travel arrangements and also put you in touch with the right department if you need an assessment of any special learning requirements that you have (if, for example, you are deaf or have dyslexia). The student welfare office is also a good place to find. These are not always well publicised, but they do a lot of work behind the scenes to help their students, and their notice board will tell you about additional student facilities, such as late-night safety buses. The Careers Advisory Service is another student service that you might need in the future, so find out now what they offer. Do they have a newsletter? Do they run courses in interview skills and CV writing? Do they have a vacancies board? You will not need some of their services until later in your course, but you might need to know about jobs in the area straightaway, and I will be discussing this in more detail in Chapter 6.

Once you have mastered your hall of residence and the main campus, take the time to stroll around the local town, especially if this is some distance from your university. It is perfectly possible (and surprisingly common) for new undergraduates whose university is not situated right in the middle of a town or city to spend the first few months of their course on campus, without once venturing beyond it. This is not necessarily a problem, although if you intend to work at some point in your first year, it is useful to have explored the town to find out what jobs might be available. It is also a good idea to have some sense of what the town has to offer. If you feel that everything is getting on top of you as the term progresses, it is nice to have found somewhere in the locality to which you can escape for a few hours.

Amongst all this walking, you will probably also be hit by the mixed delights of Freshers' Fair. This event takes on different names in different universities, but its aim is the same in all: to get new undergraduates involved in the life of the university and advise them how to make the most of their time there. New undergraduates have differing attitudes towards this event. Some feel that it is an ideal opportunity to join every club going and get involved in many of the societies and action groups that exist within the university. Some feel so intimidated by the sight of it (it is sometimes crammed into a small hall and is very noisy and chaotic), and by the fact that people might approach them to ask them to join something, that they take one look and back off. Still others have been told that it is just not the done thing to get involved. None of these responses is ideal if you are going to make the most of Freshers' Fair. The key is to know what you want from the event before you jump in. If you have come to university intending to join the rowing club, for example, then you will have a point of reference straightaway. You can go to their stall and sign up, using the chance to look around at the other stands as you go. If you have always been involved in a number of clubs or societies, you might want to join several, but if you are unsure, see this as a fact-finding exercise. You do not have to sign up to anything, but you can get leaflets about what each group does, so that when you have settled in you can think further about whether you have the time or the inclination to join up. These events do not rely solely on university clubs and societies. Information about the welfare office, the safety bus and the Careers Advisory Service will be available here, for example, so you could save yourself some time by browsing around for a while.

Once you have got through your first week, you will be ready to approach the studying, but you might also be surprised at how tired you feel. Entirely new surroundings, new people to meet, forms to complete and that uneasy sense that you might be missing something, all combine to make the first week quite an experience. You will be pleased to find in your second week that things are feeling much more familiar. You will know your neighbours in your hall, you will have established a routine of where to eat and meet people in the day, you will have made new contacts, some of whom will become friends. You will now be bombarded with reading lists, course outlines, timetables and schedules for seminar papers, presentations and essays. So too will everyone else, but it is easy to feel that everyone is coping better than you, particularly if the group of students with whom you mix includes several undergraduates who like to give the impression that they can breeze through anything. If you reach this point, hold your nerve and try not to panic. Things will become easier, but you need to have a plan. Two weeks spent in a flat spin, unsure of where you should go or what you should do, is two weeks wasted, which means more work to catch up on in the vacation.

Conquering the first six weeks should be easy, if you follow these guidelines:

- Register with your department, get your NUS card and library card, find out your password to access IT services and your email.
- Make sure that you have filled out every form that is relevant to you. If you are not sure about a form, do not ignore it, but take it to your departmental secretary and discuss what you should do next.
- Find your mail tray and check it as often as you can to make sure that you have done everything that is asked of you.
- Try not to rely on the generalised timetables given to you for each subject in the form in which you receive them; it is too easy to get confused between them. Prepare your own personal timetable, listing all your lectures and seminars, and copy it several times so that you will always know where you need to be.
- Make a study timetable as soon as you can (as outlined in Chapter 3), even if you have to make changes to it as the term progresses.
- Be clear about the options that are coming up (see Chapter 5), but also make sure that you are registered for the right options now.
- Make sure that your tutor knows about anything that might become a problem (such as times when you need to be away from university, or any other obstacles to your learning).
- Resist the temptation to file away your reading lists without first having assessed them and made some initial decisions about which books you will need in the first few weeks (see Chapter 3).
- Book onto any courses in IT or within the library system that you know you will need.
- Be clear about how you will be assessed later in the term or at the end of your current course of study (see Chapter 2).
- Work out your finances in the light of what you now know about your study commitments (see Chapter 6).
- Find out a little bit about what is happening outside your department (social events, study skills workshops, clubs and societies), even if you do not at first have time to attend them.

- If you are not sure about anything, *ask*. If you are wary of bothering your tutor, ask your departmental secretary, who will probably know everything there is to know.

This may seem like a long list, but if you take it a step at a time it will help to clarify your thoughts, keep everything on track and give you peace of mind.

▶ What can be achieved in the time available to you

One of the most disorientating aspects of moving from school or college (or a full-time job) to university is that you suddenly seem to have vast amounts of time available to you, in which you could do nothing. Whereas you might be used to a full timetable, with perhaps six or eight lessons a day, you may now find that you have only six or eight sessions of structured time in a week. This is great, in that you have more control of your time and can study in the most effective way for you, but it can be unnerving at the outset. Science undergraduates have this easier in some ways, as they usually have much fuller timetables, but as a Humanities or Social Science undergraduate you will learn to enjoy planning and managing your own time. Much of the advice offered in this book will help you with the detail of how to do this, but there are four important general points to remember:

1. By creating your own, personalised study timetable you will get a clear idea of how each week will work out. You will have decided, within the boundaries of your official timetable, what you need to achieve in each week, perhaps in each day. This will give you structure, and help you to work out whether you are keeping on track.
2. Your personalised timetable will also allow you to take care of making some structured time to relax. Balance is the key to managing your degree effectively: too much study will leave you burnt out by the end of your first year; too much leisure will result in a major panic by year three. There is a natural rhythm to the life of an undergraduate. Generally, they work hard in the first two terms, ease off a bit for the next couple of terms, get back into the routine of working hard for the next two terms (often because their overdrafts are at the limit and they cannot afford to do much socialising) and then really put in the effort for their final year. Although this rhythm may be changing with the increase in modular degrees, you will still find that you work harder in some months than in others, but, however hard you are working, you need to give yourself some time off. If you are not naturally a hard worker, you will still find

this useful advice. Students who try to avoid too much hard work often spend most of their time feeling that they should be doing something, they are always lagging behind and their leisure time is never really 'free' time. It is an irony of university life that those who work hard and then reward themselves with time off from studying are often less stressed and less likely to feel overworked and hassled than those who avoid doing too much and so always feel under pressure to catch up.

3. The third aspect of time management to remember is to work out how your finances will fit in with your studying. Your leisure time will be dictated to some extent by money (how many times a week can you afford to go out?) but this is not always the case. There are plenty of ways to give your brain a rest without spending money, but you might need to earn money however little you go out, and this needs to be built in to your plan. Chapter 6 will help you to tackle your finances in more detail but, broadly speaking, you will need to decide whether to earn money only in the vacations, at weekends, each week or for several nights in one week and then not at all the following week, if your job allows you to do this. In a related point, you might find that your social life and work life could be dovetailed to some extent (if you are working in the Union bar, for instance) and you may also have a more formalised social life (perhaps as part of a committee or as a member of a club that meets regularly) which will dictate your timetable to some extent.

4. The fourth, and perhaps the most important, aspect of time management whilst you are at university is to recognise, and appreciate, what is work and what is leisure. Sounds simple, doesn't it? But in fact it is only simple once you have learnt to understand how you work. Spending all day in the library is only 'work' if you have actually done something that represents a whole day's work. If you do not work well in a library atmosphere, finding yourself looking out of the window or reading chapters of books that are not relevant to your essay, you will have a problem. In that case, it would be far better to take the books out of the library, study them intensively for a few hours and then return them, rewarding yourself with an hour or so off in the afternoon. Similarly, if you decide to work with friends for an evening, have a plan of action ready in advance. You are going to revise so many texts, or practise a certain number of essay questions. Make sure that you do this, then you can relax and enjoy the rest of the evening. If you find that you have been staring at a blank computer screen for ten minutes, waiting in vain for inspiration, give up for the moment and take a break. However many times you tell your brain that the deadline for this piece of work is tomorrow, it is not going to get going without some outside help. Update your reading list, fill out some index cards with keywords, read a chapter of a textbook, play a

computer game – anything to get your brain warmed up and ready to tackle the essay again. Students often say that they are working really hard and just cannot get ahead, when in fact they are floundering under poor time management and so stressing themselves unnecessarily.

Once you have mastered these four aspects of time management, you will also need to accept that you cannot do everything. You can have a pretty good go at it, of course, but there will always be a book that you did not get around to finishing, a club that you never quite joined or an IT course that always seemed to be full whenever you had the time to register. Each year will feel different to you. What seemed like an impossible task in the first year will be just part of your routine by the second; you will never do it all, but that is part of student life, common to every graduate, and in the end you will feel, if you manage your time well, that you have achieved as much as you could, and more than you ever thought that you would be able to handle.

▶ Vacations and how to make the most of all that time

It can seem like a dream come true. You go to university, check out the timetable and find that you seem to have five months a year with no timetabled activities. Then comes the snag. Somehow, you have to work out how to make the most of that time: how to study effectively, earn enough cash to keep you going and take some time out for relaxation. University vacations are funny things. You can feel that you have just got going, just immersed yourself in the study for the term, and suddenly the vacation is upon you. On the other hand, some terms feel as if they are going on forever and you cannot wait to get to the end of them. Each undergraduate will differ in the amount of university work that he or she can reasonably hope to achieve in the vacations. Some departments will pile on a heavy workload for each vacation, whilst others will expect their students to do little more than catch up on their reading lists. Your vacation might disappear altogether at some points in your course if, for example, you are producing a dissertation, carrying out a work placement or studying abroad.

In addition to all these variables, you are likely to have to earn some money in the vacations, and this can make any studying a problem. Whatever your situation, there are some guidelines that you can follow so as to make the most of the time that you have available to you. You might have to begin by negotiating with your bank, your parents and anyone else involved in helping to fund your life as an undergraduate. You may then be able to decide only to work for money during the summer vacation, or that you will work at Christmas and Easter, but not in the summer. You will have a clear idea by the end of your second term just how much cash you need to raise and the guidance in Chapter 6 will help you to work out what you need to do with regard to your financial organisation, but you will have to plan some academic work for the vacation, regardless of whether you have to earn money or not, and the points outlined here will help you.

It is essential that you try to visualise the vacations as part of your course, a part that allows you to do other things (thank goodness) but one that needs to be incorporated into your overall study strategy. So, when you are drawing to the end of your term-time study plan (at the beginning of week ten of the study plan outlined in Chapter 3), you must plan your vacation-study timetable. Although some of your vacation work will be dictated by the university (if you are given essays to complete or other work to prepare for the following term, for example), but much more of the work that you hope to get through in the vacation will follow on from your term-time study plan. When you assess how well you have done in the term, be honest with yourself and realistic about what you can achieve in the vacation. There is no point in deciding that you have a huge amount of leftover reading to do and that it must all be transferred to your vacation plan; this will just leave you demoralised and even more behind at the start of the next term, unless you know that you are going to have the time to do it all. This is the time to clear out your book pile ruthlessly (as was mentioned in Chapter 3) and make realistic plans. Begin, as you did with your term-time plan, with the work that you have been set. Add to this all the additional work that you hope to do, and then add items from your 'wish list' of collating and contemplating work that you would like to finish.

I have outlined below one possible vacation timetable for the example student whose term-time study plan was included in Chapter 3. I will assume that the vacation lasts for five weeks and that, in common with most undergraduates, the student did not quite get through all the work that was incorporated in the earlier plan.

Week One: Secondary reading for English text three to be completed
Read English text six

Week Two: English practice essay to be written
Read history text six

Week Three: WEEK OFF

Week Four: Review the tutor's comments on the least successful essays
and make notes on how to improve

> Reading for next term – English texts one and two
> Reading for next term – History text one with secondary
> reading

Week Five: Assess the term's progress in all subjects
Complete index cards for revision in all subjects
Begin to plan Sociology dissertation ready for week one
supervision

As you can see, this plan feels different from the term-time plan. Your plan might be far more detailed than this and include more tasks, but for any vacation plan you need to ensure that the pace is different from term-time working, there is more space for thinking time and the vacation study differs in nature before and after the week off. The week off is vital, by the way. You need a week (and in the summer vacation longer than a week) in which to do absolutely nothing related to your studying. You will know, if you have ever learnt to play an instrument, or tried to master a difficult computer game, that you can leave it alone for a week and when you come back to it you amaze yourself at how much better you are than you were before. Our brains need a rest occasionally. The secret of success here is to make your-self take that time off, even if you are a bit behind with your timetabled study, and then equally firmly make yourself go back to work at the end of your planned time off.

We can see from this plan that our student did get a bit behind with the reading towards the end of the term and so the time before the week off in this vacation plan is spent actively producing work, such as the essay, and frantically catching up with the reading for English and History. I say 'fran-tically' because, even if the reading is not difficult in itself, it feels pressurised when you know that you are behind, and so this reading is usually done with an eye on the clock and a wish for it to be finished and out of the way. If you find yourself getting behind in your plan, make amendments to it (perhaps a little less background reading, or a reduced amount of revision work) rather than either remaining behind for the whole of the vacation, or abandoning the plan altogether. Once the reading and the essay are done (even if you read a little less than you planned), you will have the satisfac-tion of knowing that you have done all that your university expects of you in the vacation. Now you can relax.

After your week off you will feel that you are working to get ahead of your-self (and probably most of your fellow students) and so this period of work will feel much more upbeat. It is still important if you are not to be over-whelmed by week three of the following term, but it can be done with some time built in for 'idle' contemplation of your course and what you have learnt. This is usually when your best ideas will suddenly come to you as if from nowhere. It is clear from the plan that this student has had no problems keeping up with Sociology. All the set texts were read and the essay completed on time. It is for this reason that the 'advance reading' in weeks four and five is focused upon History and English, to avoid getting behind again. Sociology is not ignored however, and time has been allocated to preparing for a supervision on a Sociology dissertation. This dissertation may not be due in for several months, but the initial supervision is important, and so the student has decided to spend some time preparing for it. This is effective management, as the student is much more likely to be able to think creatively and widely at this point, before the pressure of the new term's workload begins.

Week five also includes a suggestion that index cards be completed to help with future revision. You may choose not to use index cards – maybe you just make concise notes, use spider diagrams or work out a series of practice essay plans. Whatever you do, it is far easier to condense your work into a digestible form at this stage, when you have some free time and it is fresh in your mind, rather than trying to cram it all in at the last minute. This example offers you an outline plan, and there are of course many other tasks that you might have to fit into your schedule. You might also have to condense your plan into just a couple of weeks if you are earning money in some of the vacations. During the term, if you have followed a plan similar to that given in Chapter 3, you will have taken the time to assess how well you are progressing in each of your subjects or modules and have gathered together the material that you need for the vacation. This is important if you cannot gain access to the university library for some time: photocopy articles that you will need and take out books on vacation loan, having checked that they are relevant and will be useful.

There will be other items to add to your vacation timetable, and the suggestions below can be used as a checklist to ensure that you are including everything that needs to be there:

- Do you have to arrange to meet your colleagues (perhaps not until the beginning of next term) to prepare a seminar presentation? Can you begin to work on it, perhaps having discussed via email what each member of the group will be doing?
- Do you have any research to carry out at your local library?
- Do you have to begin to arrange a work placement, or a period studying abroad?
- Do you need to study your options for next term and plan what you will be doing, perhaps after contacting your tutor via email for clarification on details of one of the courses?
- Would it be helpful to go back over your reading lists to make sure that

you have used them to best effect? Are there any books that you need to order ready for the beginning of next term?

- Is there anything that you have put to one side, sure that you will never understand it, which would be worth tackling again now that you are under a bit less pressure?
- Do you need to check out your university's Careers Advisory Service website for guidance on how to get a vacation job, or for help with your future plans?
- Do you have commitments to a club or society that could be handled in the vacation?
- Are there other peripheral sources that you would like to explore, such as catching up on films or plays that you should see, or exhibitions or conferences that you should attend?

There are plenty of other items that you will want to add to your checklist, but these will give you ideas to get you going. Time spent planning is never wasted. If you know in advance exactly what you are hoping to achieve in the vacation, and how you aim to achieve it, you will be in a much better position to enjoy the time off that you do have and to make the most of the study time that you have set aside for yourself. You will also, most importantly, feel that you are keeping ahead of expectations when you return to university.

▶ The mature student experience

In many ways the experience of being a mature student at university is no different from that of being a younger student, and, where there are differences, you will usually find that they are to your advantage. Mature students perform well at undergraduate level and the problems that you might be anticipating may well turn out to be linked to your perception of yourself as an undergraduate rather than being related to your performance or ability. It is this aspect of the mature student experience that we will address first.

You may have certain preconceptions about how you are viewed by your fellow students or your tutors (indeed, about how you should view yourself) and these can be dispelled instantly. One of the joys of going to university as a mature student is that, within days of your arrival, you will find that you are not viewed as an interloper amongst a young student group, but just as another member of that group, who will be accepted as easily as any other. You are all there for the same purpose, you are all striving to learn and achieve, and this overrides everything else. All universities have a substantial body of mature students and, on the whole, lecturers will appreciate the contribution that you have to make. When they are faced with a seminar group of resolutely silent undergraduates, it is to the mature student that they will turn for a bit of backup and cooperation. Mature students generally contribute easily to seminars and this is met with unstinting gratitude on the part of tutors who are trying to get the group working together.

When mature undergraduates are asked about their experience of university life and the problems that they have encountered, they usually look a little flummoxed, saying that they just got on with it, like all the other students, and it really did not matter at all that they were in the older age range of their studying or social circle; but this is not to say that there are not differences, and making the most of the differences will be part of the effective management of your degree. There are six areas of potential difference that you might fruitfully consider when planning your degree strategy:

1. The first area has already been mentioned: *seminars*. Of course there are mature students who do not feel any more confident about speaking out in a seminar group than their younger colleagues, but, even if this is the case, they usually feel socially obliged to help out the tutor. Many seminar groups are lively places to be, with an easy interchange of ideas, but, if you are in a group where the silence lengthens to more than 30 seconds, you may feel it incumbent upon you to say something, anything, just to get things going.

    A word of caution about seminar groups, however: you can take it too far. A study of students' reactions when faced with a seminar situation would highlight many reasons why silence sometimes prevails. It might be anxiety about saying the wrong thing, or guilt over not having read the set text. It might be simple shyness, or fear of looking too keen in front of fellow students. In some cases it simply never seems to occur to a student to speak out and the presence of a mature student in the group can in itself be intimidating for some younger students. It is the job of the tutor to overcome these hurdles, to provide interesting material and the impetus to get a good debate under way, before taking a back seat when the seminar really gets going. When it works, it is one of the greatest pleasures for a university lecturer, but it can take time. A mature student who is happy to speak out is a boon, but one who continues to give an opinion on every issue without giving anyone else the chance to work themselves up to speak can be a nightmare. So, use the same social intuition that prompted you to speak when it comes to deciding when not to speak, when to let the silence grow until someone else joins in. This will stop the seminar becoming no more than a discussion between you and the tutor. If you are concerned about whether you are saying too much or too little, have a chat with the tutor after a seminar: he or she will be honest with you about the situation and may simply beg you to keep talking.

2. The second aspect of managing your degree that may come naturally to you is the art of *networking*. You may well be used to maintaining contact with work and professional colleagues, and mature students certainly seem to have a knack for keeping in touch with every visiting speaker as well as with fellow undergraduates with whom they have worked at any point in their degree programme. It may not be a problem to you to keep in touch via email with a few lecturers from whom you have received help, but sometimes mature students who are happy to keep in touch with a wide variety of useful contacts outside university feel more hesitant about whether this is appropriate within university. It is, so make sure that the principles that you applied in your working life (maintaining useful contacts, widening your networking base at every opportunity, keeping your communication levels high) stay with you during your time as an undergraduate.

3. *Socialising* can be the greatest headache for mature students. They can feel that they are too old to go to the club night in the Union bar, but do not feel inclined to go to the debating society. If you want to do either of these things, or both of them, face it head on and go. Younger students will not care at all that you are enjoying yourself at a gig on a Friday night, watching the latest band and having a good time with them. If anything, it will break down any barriers that exist. For many mature students, the problem is not deciding which event to go to, but making the choice to go to anything at all. You are likely to be busy running a home and a family and perhaps working to earn money as well; you just do not feel that you have the time to spare to socialise. It may be that you genuinely cannot get the time to do it, but it will make an enormous difference to you if you can get to even a few social events. These do not have to be in the evening, and they do not have to be purely social. Visiting speakers sometimes stay on for a time to socialise after an event, poetry 'slam' sessions are often held at lunchtime, your university may have film screenings during the afternoon. You have come to university to study, and you are probably highly focused upon the task before you. It is difficult enough at times to keep up with the work and run a life outside university, but there is something special about attending even one social event, suddenly you feel like a 'real' student, part of an experience that is beyond the studying: you become more than just an individual getting a degree, you become an undergraduate in the widest sense. If anything is guaranteed to inspire you to keep going, that will.

4. *Mature students' groups* do a good job of supporting their members, although they are often underpublicised, so you might have to hunt to

find one on your campus. They can provide you with practical help (helping you to sort out your finances, finding creative ways of studying that allow you to satisfy all the competing demands on your time) and plenty of moral support. They also provide a good forum for meeting other mature students from a wide range of courses, which can in itself be inspiring, but socialising with your mature students' group to the exclusion of all the other opportunities that will come your way may leave you feeling isolated from your younger colleagues. If you can make the time to socialise, try to do it with a range of friends, as this will more accurately reflect your range of interests and will increase the richness and diversity of your undergraduate experience.

5. As you will discover, *time management* is an issue for most mature students. You may feel a stab of envy as you run, panting, into the coffee room two minutes before your lecture beings, having got the children to school or waited about for the plumber to fix the washing machine, only to find younger colleagues apparently unruffled by the vagaries of life, drinking their third cup of coffee. You see yourself as trying to juggle all the diverse aspects of your life, whilst others seem to have not a care in the world. There are two things to remember here. Firstly, your younger colleagues might look calm on that particular morning, but they too are probably holding down part-time jobs, or are agonising over an ever-increasing overdraft. Secondly, you have a natural advantage here. You are used to managing your time and your finances, you already have years of experience in juggling the demands that life has made upon you. What might be difficult for some younger undergraduates, such as trying to get an essay finished whilst earning money and cramming in a social life, will be easy for you. Your approach is likely to be that you have to complete a task, so you will get it done: you have been doing something similar for years. Statistically, mature students have been shown to complete their work on time more consistently than their younger colleagues, resulting in less stress in the long run, so cling to that thought as you progress through your degree.

6. In Chapter 3 much was made of the need to use *your own sources* in order to individualise your work, increase its relevance and boost your grades. As a mature student, you are in the ideal position to do this. Your previous career may be directly relevant to your current studies, and if your degree has a vocational aspect, you are likely to have studied the field widely before you even reached university, and this will motivate you, and also help you to fit what you are learning into context. Although you will want to be careful to keep the balance between academic rigour and hearsay evidence, you will have the advantage of being able to test hypotheses against your own experience, and this is especially useful in

Social Science. You will still need to undertake the challenge of testing a hypothesis, but at least you will have a reliable 'gut feeling' for whether it is likely to be accurate or require some modification.

Even if your time in the workplace is of little relevance to your undergraduate programme, you will have life experiences to offer. You will have had far more opportunity than many other students to visit the theatre or exhibitions, have undertaken part-time classes in your subject in the past, or have read widely in a range of areas. Chapter 2 stressed the need to make connections of all sorts within your studying, and mature students are well placed to do this. They tend to see life as a connected whole, and find it natural to draw parallels between one area of investigation and another. This is, of course, a generalisation, but it is worth noting because the opposite of this instinctive connectivity can happen, and again it is a problem of perception. Some mature students feel, wrongly, that now they are at university all their past life is irrelevant and should be discarded as not in keeping with their new life as an undergraduate. Try to guard against this tendency. You will want to avoid introducing personal anecdotes into each essay, or relying too heavily upon your professional experience in every presentation or seminar paper, but equally there is no need to throw away your valuable, and unique, life experience. As with so much in the effective management of your degree, creating a balance is the key to success.

These six aspects of the mature student experience will, no doubt, be only part of what makes up your life as an undergraduate. This section opened with the assertion that mature students are in most ways no different from their younger colleagues, and this statement still stands and is more important than any differences that might arise. However, if you see any differences that exist as positive (and they are) and there to be exploited, you will increase your chances of success. Whatever the differences and similarities, there is one thing that you can be sure of: you are likely to be highly motivated. Attending university, especially as a mature student, requires a high level of commitment. Just getting to this stage is an achievement, and you can ensure that it is just the first of many.

Spot guide

The key points to remember from this chapter:

- explore your hall of residence and main campus thoroughly
- book onto IT courses as soon as you can
- register with your department, the library and the NUS in the first week
- avoid ignoring forms that you are unclear about
- find your mail tray and check it frequently
- find you departmental secretary's office
- tell your tutor about any problems that you feel might hinder your learning
- go to the Freshers' Fair, even if only as a fact-finding exercise
- check out every notice board that you pass
- make your own, personalised study timetable, for both the term times and the vacations
- make sure that you are clear about the options that are coming up, as well as confirming that you are registered on the right options in the first term
- keep track of your finances, even if things are not going according to plan
- think about how you will achieve a balance between working and relaxing; be sure that you are clear about the difference between the two
- if you are a mature student, be aware of the issues that might arise for you and be reassured that they will be positive

5 Working your Options

Troubleshooting guide

Read this chapter for help in the following areas:

- if you are not sure what to expect from lectures
- if you find yourself missing lectures
- if you are confused about seminars
- if you find contributing to seminars difficult
- if you have to give a seminar paper or presentation
- if you have received a mark that you are unsure about
- if you are nervous about attending tutorials or supervisions
- if your marks are disappointing and you are not sure how to improve them
- if you are faced with first-year options
- if you are confused about the options available to you
- if you are unclear about the consequences of making course choices
- if you are doing a combined degree and are having trouble fitting all the work into the time that you have available
- if you are uncertain about how to earn money whilst studying effectively
- if you are anxious about examinations
- if you cannot decide between taking courses assessed by examinations and those that involve coursework
- if you are facing timetable clashes
- if you want to begin working towards your future career

▶ Lectures, and how to use them

Lectures provide one of the fundamental teaching blocks of the undergraduate teaching system, and yet attitudes towards them vary widely. Do not be fooled into thinking that lectures are not worthwhile. They are, and you might put yourself at a disadvantage later in your course if you get into the habit of missing them. When it comes to revising, there is nothing better than your own notes from lectures. It is inevitable that you will leave a few of your lectures with a sense of disappointment; maybe the lecturer was not very clear or inspirational, or perhaps the lecture did not cover the area that you had hoped to hear about. However, to miss lectures is usually just a way of making more work for yourself. The advantage of being there is that you can make judgements about the subject (Is it worth your while to pursue it further? Have you gained some insight into how to approach the subject?) and you will certainly save yourself a lot of reading time.

I was approached recently by a student at the end of the third seminar in a series of six. She apologised in a rather offhand way for missing my seminars and went on to explain that she had thought that they were lectures and so had not felt it necessary to turn up. My initial feelings of irritation were quickly replaced by feeling sorry for her; she really seemed to think that lectures were 'optional extras' and not something that she needed to attend. I would like to think that she had lost some valuable instruction by missing my seminars, but missing the lectures was probably a far more serious problem in terms of her time management; by the end of the term she will undoubtedly feel that there is an awful lot of work to do. Some students are not this adamant about the irrelevance of lectures, but instead try to make half an effort to attend them by leaving a tape recorder in the lecture room prior to the event, in the expectation that they will in this way be able to extract the information given in the lecture at a later time. Lecturers are quite used to speaking to a group of students and a whole pile of tape recorders, so they are unlikely to complain, but this approach is not time efficient.

There may be times when you have to be absent from a lecture and so have to rely upon a recording of the event, but if you make a habit of it, you need to examine why you are using this method. You may feel that you work better in your own time, and so this seems to be a tactic that will work. You fully intend to spend time listening to the tape, making detailed notes of what is relevant to you. This has two distinct disadvantages. The first is that you may never get around to listening to the tape; indeed, as the term progresses and the tapes mount up, this is increasingly likely to happen. Secondly, if the lecture is not very helpful to your studies, you will have wasted time listening and relistening to the tape to decide on this, whereas if you attend the lecture, you can make this judgement far more accurately and quickly. If you do have to tape a lecture, try to make sure that you also get hold of a copy of the notes from someone who was actually there. This may sound like overkill, but it is surprising how easy it is to miss the nuances of a lecture if you were not present. You can usually get hold of copies of any handouts that were given out in advance of the lecture, but the tape might not make it clear that more handouts were given out during the lecture; having a pile of missed handouts to collect over the course of a term will simply add to the pressure. If you can get notes from an active note-taker, you will also glean valuable additional information, such as asides (sometimes the most interesting thing about a lecture) that might have been missed on tape.

If you miss a lecture and have not been able to make a tape (and this will happen to every undergraduate at some point), try to make contact with the lecturer as well as borrowing the lecture notes of another student. On some courses this is easy; you may see the lecturer every week. On other courses, each lecturer will only give one or two lectures a term, and will have spent a great deal of time and effort making this rare event as useful as possible. If you speak to the lecturer concerned and explain why you were absent, you will probably find that he or she is happy to give you a copy of the lecture notes, giving you the information that you need straight from the horse's mouth.

Having (hopefully) persuaded you that attending lectures is a good idea, you now need to think about how you can make the most of them. You may have to transform yourself from a naturally passive listener to an active participant in the whole process of the lecture. You might be given a detailed synopsis of what the lecture is gong to contain in advance of the event, but more often you will just receive a title for the lecture and the details of who is to give it. In an ideal world, you will have done some prepatory reading, but this is not always possible, and lectures are designed to do much of the groundwork for you. You will receive lectures in a variety of locations, so make sure that you know where it is best to sit in each one, either with a group of friends, by the window if you find that a more inspiring place or by yourself if you find it difficult to concentrate with people close to you. Get to each lecture a few minutes early, so that you have time to set up by getting your paperwork ready, the handouts and your notebook out of your bag and the set text, if there is one, open in front of you. It will be distracting for you to have to spend time surreptitiously trying to remove rustling papers from your bag once the lecture has begun.

Once you are ready, you will not be just a passive receptor of information. The process is far more subtle than that. You will, of course, be taking notes, but they will not consist only of what is being said in the main body of the lecture. You will want to take notes of asides from the lecturer, as these often give you clues as to where to go next, clues that you will not get anywhere else. You may also hear mention of books and articles that you could use to personalise your reading lists. Perhaps the most valuable part of the lecture notes will be those notes that you have made to yourself about ideas that come to you in the lecture. This is where apparently boring or unproductive lectures come into their own. As you sit, feeling that this is not very relevant to you, you can let your mind wander a little, never straying far from the lecture in case the lecturer suddenly becomes riveting, but giving yourself the chance to add your own notes to the lecture notes.

The example below will give you an idea of how your notes might look after a lecture. I will assume for the purposes of this example that we are back with the student who appeared in Chapters 3 and 4, listening to a lecture on a poem by John Donne. The first two stanzas will serve to illustrate the active note-taking techniques that you might employ:

> Sweetest love, I do not goe,
> For wearinesse of thee,
> Nor in the hope the world can show
> A fitter love for mee;
> But since that I
> Must dye at last, 'tis best,
> To use my selfe in jest
> Thus by fain'd deaths to dye.

> Yesternight the Sunne went hence,
> And yet is here to day,
> He hath no desire nor sense,
> Nor halfe so short a way:
> Then feare not mee,
> But beleeve that I shall make
> Speedier journeyes, since I take
> More wings and spurres than hee.

I have detailed below the page of notes that you might make during the lecture. The section on the right represents the main lecture notes, taken directly from what the lecturer is saying and the handout material, while the section on the left represents your marginal notes, made as extra points occur to you whilst you are listening to the lecture.

Revise this one for the examination	• Lecture title: Donne's 'Song' • Lecturer: Dr Becker • Date: 16 October 2002
How does his work relate to Shakespeare?	• Donne was born in 1572, he died in 1631
Check out his religious poetry	• He wrote religious and secular poetry

Continued

Which other poet does this remind me of?	• His family was strongly Roman Catholic, his brother and uncle were persecuted for their faith
Check on my history notes for the period – could I use him as an example?	• He converted to the Church of England and held office as secretary to Sir Thomas Egerton
	• He secretly married Ann More, Lady Egerton's niece and this caused him problems in his career, leaving him in financial difficulty
	• He was ordained in 1615, having come to the notice of James I
My idea – could this be linked to Hardy and his poetry after the death of his wife?	• His wife died in 1617; he was deeply distressed
Check out sociology module 'Death and bereavement', maybe he could be used as an example?	• He made elaborate preparations for his death, and preached about it
Compare this poem with a couple of his religious poems	• He wrote predominantly religious poetry towards the end of his life
Find out more about the metaphysical poets. Do I understand what a metaphysical conceit is? Is George Herbert a metaphysical poet? Do not forget to refer to the speaker rather than the poet	• This poem is typical of the metaphysical poets, and includes a metaphysical conceit, as the speaker is compared to the sun, which returns each day, as he will to his love, to whom the poem is addressed
	• He is trying to calm his distressed lover, making light of his departure by jesting about his need to return, which he claims is greater than the need of the sun to return each morning

Continued

How does this compare with the war poets and their poetry about departure? My idea – could be useful for my seminar paper to compare them	• It may have been written to his wife, when he left to travel to the Continent in 1611 • Details of the poem and analysis on handout
The language and spelling is difficult to understand in places – work on several of his poems to get the hang of it	• The language is lyrical – it may have been intended to be sung – but the thoughts and ideas are complex
Check this with typical courtly love poetry. Are these genuine emotions? Didn't Shakespeare write verses to be sung? How do they compare?	• It would have been circulated in manuscript form and could be used by others in similar circumstances
Recheck my earlier notes on the manuscript tradition – this could be a good example READ THIS!	• This poem is similar in many ways to the poem 'To his coy mistress' by Andrew Marvell, with its jesting tone and darker undertone

Although you would hope that the lecturer said much more than this in the time available, you can see from this example that the student has done as much work as the lecturer. The marginal notes join with the lecture notes to give valuable extra information and lead the student into further relevant areas of study. Several points are worth noting:

• The lecturer's name is important, as is the date of the lecture – it will remind you where this lecture fitted into your overall programme of study and who to approach if you have any further queries.

• The student has decided at the outset to revise this poem for the examinations, so these notes will be kept for revision and easy reference in essays.

• Several of the notes are making links to work in other subjects; these links need to be noted as soon as they strike you, as they are easily forgotten after a lecture. They will provide impressive material for coursework and examinations.

• Note that sometimes the notes are just queries, reminding the student to look things up later.

• In the case of 'metaphysical poets' and 'metaphysical conceits', the student has clearly been left in some doubt as to what the phrases mean. This can happen, and noting your confusion in the margin like this will keep you from panicking, and remind you to do some more work on areas of confusion, either by further reading or bringing the matter up at your next seminar on the subject.

• The student has had problems in the past remembering to refer to the speaker in a poem rather than assuming that the poet is speaking personally. By making a note of it here, and each time that it crops up, the habit of using the correct terms will begin.

• If you are faced, as this student was, with language that is difficult, either because it is poetic or you are confused by the terminology, a marginal note will remind you to look at the language in the future, perhaps before the next lecture.

• Note how the student has marked several notes as 'my idea'. It is unnerving to find yourself with a brilliant idea that is perfect for the essay you are writing, but to be unsure whether it is your brilliant idea or one supplied by the lecturer. By making it clear in marginal notes like this, you can use it as your own with confidence.

• By making capitalised marginal notes of any reading that you need to do, you can go back through your notes at the end of the day at some speed in order to add to your personalised reading list. When you have done that, you can take the time, perhaps every week, to work through your lecture notes to make sure that they are clear, and check out your marginal notes to decide what action to take next so as to build upon what might have been a passive lecture and turn it into a plan of action, with links made to other modules, ideas to be included in essays, points of discussion for seminars and reading to help support your studies.

This might seem like an awful lot of hard work, but it is far easier to work hard like this during the lecture than to try to gather all this information and think of all these connections and ideas on your own. Active participation in lectures will save you time and effort and this is time that can then be spent on managing all the other aspects of your degree effectively.

▶ Seminars, and how to use them

The format and purpose of seminars were discussed in Chapters 2 and 4: they are usually the second building block in your study experience and as important as lectures. They are, however, very different from lectures. They usually consist of a group of students being brought together under the guidance of a tutor to discuss a variety of subjects. You will be a member of several seminar groups at each point in your undergraduate life and they will all differ from each other in one way or another. Some will be very demanding, if, for example, you are asked to give several seminar papers or presentations during the term, others will be far easier. You might find that the lectures for a course are scheduled to run for several weeks before the seminars begin, but if you are ready for this it should not faze you. Whatever is required of you, there are four points to remember:

1. The first thing to recognise about seminars is that your absence will be noticed. If you have to spend time away from university, it is far better to miss a lecture than your seminars. If you are missing from lectures occasionally, nobody is likely to notice, unless you have a very small lecture group. If you are absent from a seminar, your tutor will not only notice, but will also endeavour to find out what happened to you, checking at that stage whether you have been spotted at lectures – not a good position to be in.

2. From your point of view, seminars are time-savers. Although it might seem easy to miss out on a seminar, what you will miss, and what you cannot easily get in any other way, is a 'feel' for a subject. By engaging with the tutor on a topic, you will get instant feedback on which theories are discredited and which texts are most useful. You will also be able to get a sense of how others are approaching a subject area. You can decide whether this is a subject that you want to pursue further, or whether the taster of the seminar is enough to place the topic in the bottom ranks of areas that you will revisit. The tutor will show you how a text or theory fits into your course and will be able to give you some indication of how vital the text could be in examinations.

3. There is another way in which seminars can offer you shortcuts. If you are struggling with piles of statistics, for example, the overview offered by the tutor, or your fellow students, can point you in the right direction. Other students may be giving a seminar paper on a topic that you have not yet had time to tackle, thus giving you a head start when you come to approach it. The tutor will be able to share information with you that is not always given in departmental notices, such as whether a course that you are interested in is usually oversubscribed, or how to combine

the texts on your course to best effect in the examinations. If you are unclear about how to begin the preparations for an essay or dissertation, your early talks may be with your seminar tutor and this will save you the effort of wading through a long reading list, trying to find the perfect secondary text to use in order to support the argument that you want to make. Weaknesses in your study skills will become apparent to you (although not to everyone else) during seminars, and talking to your seminar tutor at the end of the seminar will provide you with an immediate source of help.

4. The last thing to bear in mind about seminars is that they offer you a 'safe' environment in which to try out ideas. If you are giving a seminar paper or presentation, you will be concerned to get it right, to be sure of yourself before you begin and will prepare for the event as if you were submitting an essay for marking. However, much of your time in seminars will be spent listening to the tutor and other students and adding ideas and observations of your own, and this is where seminars can be most useful. Even if only a couple of students in the group speak out, the seminar will work well. The marginal notes that you make in lectures will remind you of areas about which you are unsure and will help you to form questions for seminars. A supportive tutor will be able to guide you here and will be pleased with the effort that you have made to keep up with the subject. If you have covered the reading in advance, you will obviously be in a good position to contribute and ask relevant questions, but the most valuable insights that you can glean from a seminar are often entirely unplanned. You listen to the comments of the other members of the group and add your own views, or hazard an idea, and the tutor will be able to either confirm that you are on the right lines or put you straight if you are wide of the mark.

It is this last feature of seminars that leads to the two golden rules of making the most of seminars: try never to miss a seminar, and speak out as often as you can. You may not think at this stage that you will miss seminars, but it is easy to be put off if you have not done the reading that is required in advance of the event. What generally happens is that you make a note of what you are meant to be reading, fully intending to cover it before the next seminar, and then you either forget all about it until it is too late, or you find that everything else crams in on you and you run out of time to do it. In an ideal world, every student would have done every scrap of reading before each seminar, but tutors are well aware that some students in each seminar will not have done this reading and will tend to avoid making students feel uncomfortable. It is more practical to go to the seminar, even if you feel as if you are making notes on thin air about something that you have not read, than to miss the seminar and then have to cope with the reading at a later stage, as well as feeling that you have missed out on the instruction offered at the seminar. If you are behind with your reading, a seminar can be useful in pointing out approaches that you might take when you do catch up with your reading schedule. You will usually find that you can make a contribution to the seminar, even if you have not completed all the reading, so it will not be a disaster.

Speaking out at seminars comes easily to some students, but for others it is a real challenge. If you have to give a seminar paper or presentation, the decision is made for you (you are unlikely to escape by missing one of these seminars: your tutor will just reschedule), but as a member of a discussion group your participation will hopefully go beyond this. There are several reasons why you might find speaking in seminars difficult. Maybe you feel intimidated by an especially vocal member of the group, who seems determined not to let you get a word in edgeways. Perhaps you just feel shy in a group with which you are unfamiliar, or you find it difficult to think on your feet, preferring to take your time in coming up with ideas and working through them fully before you venture an opinion. Seminars will be useful to you, even if you say nothing, but speaking in seminars is an important aspect of managing your degree and building your confidence because, by engaging in the debate that is going on, you can get the most out of it and help yourself to feel less nervous when the time comes for you to give a paper. If you find yourself sitting silent in all your seminars, the way to overcome the fear is to choose which seminar group and tutor you feel most comfortable with and then to prepare for a seminar thoroughly. Read the text, do any background reading and then formulate an idea in advance that you would like to share with the group. If this sounds too daring, you could try forming a question that you think will be of interest to the other members of the group and that you know has not been covered in the lectures. Once you have broken the ice and spoken for the first time in one of your seminars, it will never seem so daunting again, and each time you make a contribution to the group, you will find it easier. If you still find yourself tongue tied, try speaking to the tutor after the seminar. Tutors often make sure that they leave a few spare minutes at the end of seminars so that students can talk to them individually, so make the most of them.

Most graduates, when asked about their degree course, reply without hesitation that seminars made up the bulk of their learning experience. If it works well (and this is largely within your control), you will be able to try out ideas in a familiar setting, get invaluable clues as to where to go next in your studying, gain support from other students and develop as an undergraduate, all under the guiding hand of a supportive tutor. If this happens, seminars are not just essential tools in your learning experience, they can also be enjoyable.

▶ What do the marks mean?

Marking for undergraduate work can be rather muddling, so it is worth pursuing your marks as you get them, finding out what they mean and discovering how you can improve upon them. Chapter 2 dealt with different methods of assessment, but the marks can come to you in a variety of forms, whatever the method of assessment being used. You might be graded by percentage, or given a mark of A, B, C and so on, and you are probably used to this style of marking from your time at school or college. You might find, particularly in your first few terms, that your marks are much vaguer, perhaps just a pass, a marginal pass or a fail (sometimes denoted by a confusing choice of letters that seem to have little to do with these words). In later work you might be told the class of degree that you could gain with the standard of work you are producing. The key is to find out, without any doubt, what the lecturers are trying to tell you. Some lecturers use their own system of marking with little reference to others, so this is an important area to demystify. If you are given a class mark (1st, 2:1, 2:2, 3rd), you will be clear, although you will need to be sure about whether the marker is saying that your essay as it stands is worthy of that class, or whether you are showing the potential to gain that class by the end of your course.

If you are given a percentage, it is usually relatively easy to find out what class of degree this would equate to, and this is also true of marks of A, B, C and so on, although you will need to make sure that the marker agrees with your assessment of what the mark means. If you are in the early stages of your undergraduate programme, you might be given a mark of pass, or more confusingly you are given a marginal pass; you will need to discover what implications this may have for your degree progression. If the mark is being given for a practice piece of work, the mark is unlikely to have any long-term effect, except on rare occasions when the examiners are undecided about where to place you for your final coursework or examination, and this should be made clear to you as you hand work in for assessment. If, however, you are given a marginal pass for a piece of coursework or the final examination in a module, you may find that this restricts the choices that you can make over later modules, and again you will need to be clear about this.

The easy way to resolve all these potential areas of confusion is to talk to the lecturer who marked your work. Sessions set aside for these discussions are usually a routine part of the life of a department. They might be called tutorials, supervisions or essay-reading sessions, but they all serve the same purpose. They give you the opportunity to discuss what you have produced with the person who has marked the work. They are not compulsory in all cases, but it could be disastrous for you to miss the chance to discuss your work in this way, as there is no other easy way to get clear guidance. These sessions are sometimes held between the marker and a pair of students. This saves the lecturer time and, it is hoped, will encourage a discussion and a less formal atmosphere. You might be asked to go along and read your essay out loud, so that the lecturer can make comments as you read, or you may be involved in a more general discussion of the subject. You will not necessarily be given a specific time to attend, but rather be told that a certain hour has been set aside by the lecturer in which to discuss essays.

Whatever form these sessions take, make sure that you are as well prepared as you can be. If this is to be the first time that the lecturer hears the essay, be ready with questions about areas where you feel unsure of your ground. If the lecturer has already marked the essay, use a highlighter pen to mark the comments that you do not understand (or cannot read) and be sure to raise these points. Crucially, do not shy away from questioning what the mark means. This is always a scary moment. You have been given a mark of 2:1, which you are hoping was sneaking its way up to a 1st, and you are dreading the lecturer telling you that, in fact, you only just scraped it up to a 2:1 and your next mark is likely to be a 2:2. Of course this will not happen. The lecturer will explain to you how the mark was arrived at and give you guidance as to how you might develop. Once you have plucked up the courage to ask in detail about your mark, you will find the rest of the session much easier.

It is the fate of most undergraduates to receive a disappointing mark for at least one piece of work in their course. This is not necessarily a bad thing. If you have not researched the topic thoroughly, or have failed to follow instructions, then these problems are easily solved in the future. If, on the other hand, you have tried out a theory that, with hindsight, you can see did not work out, or if you have missed out a major aspect of the topic of which you were entirely unaware, then try not to panic. Trying out theories (even if they did not work) and arguing your case (even if you cannot sustain it in the face of a stronger argument) is part of being an undergraduate. The most impressive of academics have been through this and emerged unscathed and you will too, as long as you make it part of your learning experience. This is, naturally, the one tutorial that you would like to miss, but do not lose heart. You may well find that the marker is as keen to see you as you are to avoid the experience; the whole piece of work will not be a catastrophe, and you will feel much better once you have discussed it and discovered which aspect you missed or which argument did not hold up under scrutiny.

Individual sessions with lecturers to discuss your marks can be amongst the most challenging situations that you will find yourself in, particularly in your early days as an undergraduate, and you will feel nervous, particularly if you are talking to an unfamiliar lecturer. You may have produced an essay in the peace of your own room, enjoying the process of articulating your thoughts and forming your arguments. You might now feel that you are having to defend that work, although this is not how it will seem to you once you are actually in a discussion with the marker. Tutorials may be challenging, at least in prospect, but they are also rewarding. They give you the chance to discuss your approach to a topic, tackle questions of style and methodology and, most importantly, gain in confidence in what you are trying to do. You are not expected to be perfect; just improving and learning as you develop into a more experienced and knowledgeable undergraduate.

▶ Making choices

When you begin university, you may find yourself faced with a seemingly bewildering array of choices, all of which have to be made within a relatively short space of time. Of course, you will have made some major choices at the time of applying to university and your degree may dictate the choices that you make now, but for many students the first few terms are a time when they can spread their wings academically, by choosing to take other courses in addition to their 'core' areas of study. If, for example, you are taking a Law degree, you will be committed to undertaking primarily Law courses, with maybe just one other course, whereas if you are taking an English degree, you might be offered the chance to take two other courses, with choices as diverse as Archaeology and Philosophy.

There is an argument that suggests that all choices in the early stages of your degree should be made simply on the basis of what interests you most. You may, for example, be undertaking a degree in History, but feel that an early course in Sociology would be of interest as you have never experienced that subject before, and that a course in French would help you to continue to develop the skills that you acquired at school, college or within your working life. This approach will ensure that you enjoy your studying, but there are other aspects to the decision-making that you might like to consider. Firstly, make sure that you find out as much as you can about the subjects on offer, not just the topics to be covered, but also the requirements in terms of workload and assessment. This can be a tricky task if you are expected simply to attend a half-hour briefing in each subject before making your choices, but by having some questions ready you can get hold of the information that you need. How many essays, and of what length, will be required of you? Is there a coursework element to assessment, or is this confined to examinations? Are there written details available of exactly what will be covered in the course? Do you understand what these topics involve?

Taking a risk at this stage can be fun, but only if it is a calculated risk. You will not want simply to repeat work that you have already done at pre-university level, so tackling a subject that is new to you in all or some of the areas that are covered will be invigorating, but on the other hand you do not want to be overburdened in your overall course profile. If you are unsure about an area, speak to the tutor who is advocating the course, to see if you can get some clarity into the picture. If you know anyone who has already done the course, you can get all the insider information that you need to make the right choices. You will also need to understand the type of work involved in a subject. An English course might be a 'whistle-stop tour' through English literature over the last 400 years, when what you actually enjoy is modern novels. A Sociology course might appear to deal with fascinating social issues, but if it is overly based on statistics, you need to be aware of this. The workload is going to be affected by methods of assessment. You might want to take a heavily essay-based course such as History, combined with a more diverse course such as a language or Art History.

Courses can also complement each other in terms of your workload. A course in Greek Philosophy, for example, might be useful in supporting a course in Classical Studies. A course in English Literature might support a course in American Studies. A course in Sociology might support a course in Modern History. As well as considering how these early courses might support each other, it will also help you if you are able to work out how your degree course might fit together as a whole. Many universities, if they offer this diversity of choice in the early stages of a degree, fully intend that you can enjoy your early courses and then leave them behind as your degree progresses, in which case your early decisions will be of little or no consequence from that point of view. However, it is a good idea at least to consider how courses taken at this stage might help you later on. So, for example, a degree in English might be supported by an early course in Classical Studies, if this includes a study of the work of Greek and Roman playwrights and poets. A degree in Sociology might be supported by an early course in Statistical Techniques.

One of the more difficult things to find out is how arduous an early course is likely to be in terms of the expectations placed upon you. If you ask any group of third-year undergraduates about the early courses they took, they will usually give an immediate, and vociferous, response. They will be able to tell you if a department is known for 'hard' marking in the examinations at the end of their early courses, or whether one subject is known as being much less exciting than it at first appears. They will also let you know what they enjoyed, and how they benefited from their early courses. This information is not readily available, of course, but if you can make contact with more advanced undergraduates before making your choices, this will be to your advantage, always bearing in mind that each student is different, and what might drive one student mad will make another blissfully happy.

Students do drop out of university because their courses are not as they had hoped and expected them to be, but, as with all choices at university, nothing is necessarily irredeemable until you decide that you have devoted too much time to a course to make changes. If you begin on a course in these early stages and you find that, by the second week, you absolutely hate all aspects of it, then speak to your tutor and try to make changes. This should be possible, as long as you are willing to put in the extra work to catch up with another course. Before you take this step, however, speak to a tutor on the course about why you are unhappy; it might be that the course is going to develop in a way that you will find much more amenable. Whatever choices you make, these early terms will be your chance to stretch your talents, to learn new techniques of analysis and new ways to express yourself, and there is something very satisfying about finding, in your final year, that you can turn back to these early courses and find something of relevance in them for your later study.

▶ **Further choices**

A degree course can sometimes feel like a never-ending series of decisions, each nerve-wracking in itself and together representing the profile of your degree. A History degree at one university will be markedly different from a History degree taken elsewhere, and an important aspect of managing your degree will be making sure that the choices you make create the degree which suits you best and, for most students, will help you most effectively into you chosen career. Luckily, the decision-making process will be spread over the whole of your degree, so you will not have to make irrevocable choices in your first term, and then find yourself locked into a degree course that does not reflect your interests and talents as they evolve.

The first thing to do is to find out when you will have to make choices. You might, for example, have to decide upon the overall structure of your degree after the first two terms, or perhaps make some provisional decisions as soon as you begin your course. Although you will be able to make changes, even if you have had to indicate your provisional choices early on, it is a good idea to spend time in the early stages deciding on what modules will suit you best. The early choices discussed above will tend to be based upon your interests and, perhaps, their relevance to your core subject. For later modules, you will want to take into account other issues. If you are taking a vocational degree, you may want to include a module that is purely for interest, so as to bring diversity into your university experience. If you chose your degree subject for reasons other than your possible future career, it will be worth considering some modules that lend themselves to a more work-based experience, so as to boost your CV. Chapter 6 includes an exploration of opportunities at university beyond your core degree, but within your degree you can spread your studying experience very widely. Try not to close your mind to possibilities that exist in departments other than your own. Students often find the idea of taking a module in another department quite daunting, but it can open up new ways of studying and fresh opportunities. These modules might not be well advertised in your own department, but they are worth searching out, in case you find something that appeals to you.

Working out a degree profile that combines complementary options is a constructive way of managing your degree. I have taken, for the purposes of the example below, a student taking an English degree that contains, in the main course, nine modules, four of which are compulsory:

Compulsory modules
- Shakespeare Studies
- Renaissance Literature
- Eighteenth-century Literature
- Romantic Poetry

Optional modules chosen
- Drama: this supports the Shakespeare course in general and one of the plays studied on the course is *Othello*. The Eighteenth-century Literature course is based primarily upon poetry and novels, so studying this course will allow the student to show knowledge of the plays of the period as well.
- Pinter and his Plays: this highly specialised course allows the student to advance in the study of drama, using the knowledge gained from both the Drama and the Shakespeare course.
- The Novel: this course could stand alone, but it will underpin the 'development of the novel' section of the Eighteenth-century Literature course.
- Women Writers and Feminist Criticism: again, this course is a free-standing option, but some of the novels being studied in this module are the same as those studied in The Novel course, reducing the workload of each module.
- Italian Literature: this course is taken in another department, but the works are studied in translation and the student will be able to use the study of Italian Renaissance texts to support the study of the English Renaissance.

Naturally, you will make choices based upon your interest and abilities, and there is little to be gained from choosing a module purely on the basis that it supports another and will therefore reduce your overall workload, but it is worth thinking about how much easier a degree course such as this would be in comparison to a course that contained very diverse modules, none of which related in any way to each other.

There is no need to feel that you are making these choices in isolation. Each student will have individual needs, and it is part of your personal tutor's role to guide you through the decisions that you make. You will be talking to your fellow students about what to do, but try not to be put off a particular course just because a colleague finds it unappealing: be clear about the sort of work that you enjoy and the subject areas that are of most interest to you. Again, talking to undergraduates in their later years will be helpful when you are considering the options that are available. Making these choices can be difficult, but the options open to you represent one of the most exciting aspects of university life. As you explore your options, you will begin to feel as if your degree is made up of a multiplicity of modules, all laid out on a plate waiting for you to enjoy them.

▶ Coursework versus examinations

You will probably already know, by the time you reach university, whether you produce your best work in examinations or coursework. Your undergraduate course will, inevitably, require you to succeed in both forms of assessment. The information given out to you will make it clear whether the work that you do on a course is to be assessed by examination, coursework or a combination of both, so you will be left in no doubt as to what is expected of you. Try to avoid making a choice based purely on the means of assessment for a module. You will be aware of it, of course, but, unless you are completely terrified of examinations and know that your whole course will be overshadowed by the fact that they are looming, there is nothing to be gained by avoiding all optional courses that are assessed by examination only. It is better to do the courses that you will enjoy and in which you can succeed and then sign up to one of the many study skills workshops that are available at universities. These study skills courses tend not to exist in schools, and so you are unlikely to have received specialist help such as this before. You will find that, once you have practised your examination technique and learnt how to achieve under pressure, you will be relieved that you chose the right course for you, regardless of the method of assessment.

Having made that point, you do need to be aware of the timing issues involved in choosing between modules that include coursework and those that end in examinations. Find out, if coursework is to be handed in for a module, exactly when the deadline will be. Although this can seem premature when you are near the beginning of your course, it will allow you to plan, perhaps even to modify, your choices based upon the workload that will be involved. If, for example, two of your compulsory courses end in an examination, you will need to know whether the coursework for an optional module is due in the week before those examinations. If this is the case, you will need to consider how well you will cope with revising and producing a piece of coursework at the same time, and you might have to plan your time so as to ensure that the coursework is handed in early so that you have enough time to revise. Sometimes coursework for a module is completed many weeks ahead of the examinations for other courses that began at the same time, and this gives you the advantage of getting a course 'out of the way' in advance of your preparations for the examinations. Do not forget that coursework will often be produced largely as a result of your own individual study, so you will have to manage your time well, whereas examinations have the advantage of largely managing your time for you. You have an examination timetable, and you simply have to walk into the examination room and perform well for a set period of time, rather than extending the work that you produce for assessment over several weeks or months. As with much of your university life, a balance needs to be reached, one that gives you the advantage.

▶ Practicalities in making choices

In a perfect world, the decisions about the choices that make up your degree profile would be based upon nothing more than your interests. However, for most students timetabling is important. If you know that you are useless at coping with work first thing in the morning, you might be wary of a module that has 9 o'clock lectures throughout the course. Although you might tell yourself that this is a flimsy basis on which to make a choice, you have to be honest with yourself about how you work, when you work well and when you can be fairly sure you will find it difficult to turn up and be attentive.

More common timetable problems come with modules that are held in different departments. The departments concerned will be aware of potential clashes, and this is a good reason to register your interest in a module as early as possible, even if you later find that you have changed your mind. It is vital that you tell your department as soon as you have made your choices, and certainly by the deadlines that you have been given for registering on different modules. There are always some students who turn up at the departmental secretary's office two weeks after the deadline and are then confused and disconcerted to find that their first-choice modules are already full and they will have to make compromises. To avoid finding yourself in this frustrating situation, keep in contact with your department. Even if you are not entirely sure about your choices, fill out the forms; it is far better to return a form that shows where you are in your decision-making than to neglect to do anything, leaving everybody in the dark.

On a more pragmatic level, you might need to consider the fact that you have to earn money whilst you are at university. This will not, hopefully, have to be your first consideration, but if you intend to work during the week, you might find it better to choose courses that tend to 'cluster' their lectures together on certain days, leaving you time to study by yourself on other days, or earn money. This need not necessarily be a disadvantage. If you know, for example, that you study especially well on a Saturday because you like to have a clear run at a subject and work into the evening, it may be better for you (timetable allowing) to earn money on a Monday afternoon and evening and then to make Saturday a study day.

When you are considering the timing of lectures and seminars, make sure that you are clear about the location of the sites where these will take place. If your university campus is very large and scattered, with lectures being held in buildings a mile or so apart, you might have the problem of dashing from a lecture that is supposed to end at 10.50 to a seminar that is due to begin at 11.00 on the other side of the campus. This should not put you off choosing a course, but you will need to make contingency plans. Enthusiastic lecturers do sometimes run over time, so let the lecturer who is giving the 10 o'clock lecture know that you will have to leave at 10.50; this should help to focus the lecturer back into the proper time frame. If you are giving a seminar paper in the 11 o'clock seminar, it might be a good idea for you to ask a friend to take notes for you in the earlier lecture, perhaps backed up with a recording of it, so that you can concentrate on your seminar paper. You will also need to let the seminar tutor know what is going on. Not only will this explain why you keep turning up late and breathless to the seminar, it is often possible to change the time of a seminar, particularly if several members of the seminar group are all facing the same problem.

Less obvious than timetable clashes are the potential problems of the expectations that will be placed upon you as you begin a course. If you are joining a course that assumes a level of existing knowledge, make sure that you are clear as to what is expected of you. You need not be put off if you have never studied the subject before, but you will need to talk to the tutor who is running the module so that you can find out what to read in advance of the course. The teaching style employed on the module might also be important to you. It is highly unlikely that you will reject a module simply because you find one of the lecturers hard to understand, but you might want to prepare more thoroughly for the lectures and seminars held by that lecturer so that you can keep up without it becoming a problem. Some courses will be taught entirely by seminar, so all your tuition will be received in a small group situation, with a great deal of input from the members of the group and plenty of opportunity to voice your opinions and try out your ideas. On most courses, there will be a combination of lectures and seminars, but other study situations might involve the use of guest speakers, experts in their field, or placements that require you to work outside university, sometimes for an extended period of time. All these options offer you an exciting range of choices, allowing you to study in a variety of ways with a diversity of experts – one of the pleasures of being an undergraduate.

▶ Combined degrees

Although degree courses are becoming ever-more diverse, you will probably be studying either one or two main subjects. If you are undertaking a degree in two subjects, many of your decisions will be far easier to make. You will have core modules in each subject which will occupy most of your timetable. This will not exclude the possibility of extending your studies beyond these core courses, or even beyond your two departments, but timetabling is likely to dictate much of what you do. The key to successfully managing a combined degree is threefold: you have to be firm about what you can and cannot do in the time available; you need to ensure that the lines of communication between your two departments remain open; and, finally, you must create a support network for yourself, both academically and socially.

There is a natural tendency for each department to see the world only in terms of the work that it is doing and the requirements that it places upon its students. This can lead to combined-degree students feeling that, rather than a 50:50 split between departments, they are expected to complete two thirds of a degree in each. There is no way that you can avoid this entirely, but it need not be a problem. It is difficult, if you are working with a group of single-degree students, to keep reminding them (and your tutors) that you do have other commitments elsewhere, but if you avoid taking a stand, you could find yourself swamped with work. Try to remember that your lecturers and seminar tutors in one department will not always be clear about the demands being placed upon you in your other department, and just by letting them know what is going on you can solve a lot of problems without too much trouble. If you are giving a seminar presentation in one department in the third week of term, for example, it is perfectly possible (and from the tutor's point of view, desirable) for your seminar presentation in the other department to be moved towards the end of term. As long as your lecturers know about clashes as they arise, they can help. This is particularly true if you are able to show them a personalised study timetable, demonstrating that you are organised and motivated and can achieve your best with their support.

Although departments are used to working together with students who are undertaking combined degrees, or who are taking just one or two modules in another department, it is better that you take control of the situation rather than leaving it up to your departments' secretaries or your lecturers and hoping for the best. If you have a long-term timetable clash, either in terms of lectures, seminars or coursework, make sure that you are the one to take responsibility and make the staff aware of the problem. Similarly, if you are expected to produce a joint dissertation, make sure that each department is actively involved in the process. This might simply be a case of making sure that your supervisor in each department is aware of the existence of his or her counterpart, but it might also mean that you have to arrange for supervisions with both tutors present. If you have to fill out paperwork and are not sure which department to return it to, take two copies, keep the original and hand in one copy to each department. In this way, there can be no confusion about what you are doing, where you are doing it and what you are expecting to achieve during your course.

Forming a support network when you are doing a combined degree will be essential. Although it may take a little time and effort at the beginning of your course, it will repay your efforts. Find out if there are other students who are taking the same combination as you, and make sure that you meet up with them outside your lectures and seminars. Even a meeting twice a term will be valuable in terms of helping you to catch up with any work that you have missed, discuss coursework, address any problems that you are all experiencing and offer each other support in your work. If you can find one student with whom you work well, you will be able to form a 'study pair', whereby each of you ensures that you both have the notes to every lecture, the administrative details of your courses and the material to produce the coursework. These pairings are usually very successful at university; they are not intended to allow you to do only half the work whilst relying upon your partner to do the rest, but they do provide a safety net for you in case things go wrong and, if nothing else, your study partner will be able to confirm with you that you have the times of lectures correctly copied down, or the correct deadline for coursework in your study timetable.

When you are dashing between departments, it is easy to feel that you do not have the time to socialise with the students in either department. You will have your own circle of friends, none of whom may be studying the same subjects as you, but it is worth attending at least one or two more formal social events with each of your departments. You will find that your face fits more easily into your course, you will have the chance to talk to your lecturers outside the formal learning situation and you will gain insight into how each subject is developing for everyone else. In this way, you will be bolstering your support network and so increasing your chances of gaining a good degree at the end of your studies.

▶ Choosing for the future

Chapter 6 includes details of some of the opportunities that university offers you beyond your core studying, but it is a good idea to consider, when you are contemplating your module options, how your choice might affect your future career. Some undergraduates begin university with a very clear idea of where they intend to be in five years' time. Others have no idea at all. For most, a career choice is vaguely in their view, but they are open to lots of possibilities and are hoping to explore some of these choices during their time at university. Relatively few students begin university with the firm intention of going on to take a higher degree (an MA or MSc, for example), although some will have ideas about further training that they might need, such as a postgraduate teaching course. As they progress through their course of study, however, a few students who never had any idea of continuing in their education past degree level begin to feel that postgraduate research is a good idea.

If you find yourself in this position, try not to be too hesitant about discussing your future academic options with your personal tutor. Although your tutor is unlikely to push you too firmly in one direction or another, it is useful to know as early as possible whether there is anything that you can do to help you in a future academic career. It may be that your choice of module options will be modified as you develop an interest in a particular aspect of your field, or you might want to opt for a dissertation (if this is not already compulsory) so as to gain some experience in a more extended piece of research work. You may feel shy about approaching your tutor in this way, but you should get a sympathetic response to your questions and solid, practical support as to how you can boost your chances of success in the future.

If you have a career in mind, try to explore every avenue that you can find. If you think that your first job is likely to involve giving presentations, get some practice in now by giving as many seminar presentations as possible. If you are on a course where you are given the chance to do a work placement, work with your tutor to make the placement as relevant as possible to the career that you are hoping to enter when you graduate. If you know that a language will be useful to you, enrol on a language course in addition to your core studying. Before you feel the pressure of approaching graduation, take the time to visit your Careers Advisory Service. You might not want to be bothered with a formal interview at this stage, but you can review the range of information that they can offer, such as telephone numbers for local employers offering vacation work (and work or study placements), details of extracurricular courses within the university, vacancies bulletins and information about further research options after graduation. Your Careers Advisory Service will also arrange recruitment fairs during the year. Again, go along to these to browse before you have to get too serious about your career. If you feel that the pressure is off you, you can enjoy just looking around, seeing which firms are employing graduates and what they have to offer. You will find this a motivating experience, reassuring you that there is life after graduation and it is there for the taking.

Spot guide

The key points to remember from this chapter:

- attend as many lectures as you can; try to avoid relying upon tape recordings
- get several sets of notes to copy from if you miss a lecture
- be an active listener and note-taker at lectures
- pluck up the courage to speak out in seminars
- try not to miss seminars, even if you have not done the reading
- be clear about your marks and what they mean
- take a positive and active approach to tutorials and supervisions
- do as much research as you can before you make your early choices
- make choices that fit in with your timetable, study routine and the overall profile of your degree
- if you find examinations difficult, get the help that you need rather than avoiding the problem
- if you are doing a combined degree, make sure that your support structures are in place and you keep the lines of communication open
- take advantage of what your university has to offer in terms of your future career

6 Beyond the Studying

Troubleshooting guide

Read this chapter for help in the following areas:

- if you are not sure how to make the most of your peer groups
- if you would like the support of a study group
- if you are given the chance to go on a career or study placement
- if you are not sure how to approach a placement
- if you need extra support when you are on a placement
- if you have no detailed financial plan in place
- if you are getting into financial difficulties
- if you are considering working to raise some extra cash
- if you are unclear about the best sort of paid work to do
- if you want to link your undergraduate employment to your future career
- if you need extra help with study skills
- if you need to use extra resources and equipment
- if you are wondering whether to go to an academic conference
- if you are considering getting involved in undergraduate counselling
- if you want to know more about becoming involved in:
    your university newspaper
    working in schools and colleges
    extracurricular courses at university
    information technology courses
    language courses
    creative writing courses
    study trips in departments other than your own

▶ **Peer group pressure**

Peer group pressure is usually given a bad press: it is assumed that friends are likely to distract you from your work and cause you to underachieve. However, at university peer groups can be a good thing, as long as you learn how to manage them effectively. The secret is in the balance. There are five main types of peer group with which you might be involved, and I will discuss each in turn.

Your social peer group

These are the friends that you are bound to make at university. They may have nothing to do with your course; indeed, it is helpful to have a group of friends who are not on your course. In this way you can escape from work when you need to and forget the pressures of studying for a while. This group will offer you reassurance. Although your friends may not be studying your subjects, they will all be experiencing some of the same challenges as you, and can share their solutions with you, or just join in when you want to moan about your workload. It is also only natural to enjoy hearing about someone else's efforts to get a project completed on time when you have just handed yours in: it will add to your sense of achievement.

Problems only tend to arise with this group if you let it have too great an impact upon your work routine. You have decided to spend the evening working and you get a phone call inviting you out. It is difficult to avoid the temptation, so you go and then wake up the next morning in a panic over the work that you have missed. This need not be a disaster. If you have a personalised study timetable, it should be possible for you to be flexible about your studying, going out one night and making up the work the next day. As long as you are back on track by the end of the week, no harm is done.

The second problem with this peer group and your studying is more insidious. If you are in a group where everyone seems to be breezing through their degrees, you can find yourself feeling inadequate, unable to perform as well as them and still go out five nights a week. Do not trust your first impressions in this situation; find out what is actually going on. There is always an element of competition at university: not just to get the best results, but also, in some cases, to show how little work you apparently have to do in order to get those results. Perhaps some members of your social group have far less demanding degree programmes than you; maybe you have to work to earn money and they do not; perhaps they are working well into the night on those nights that they stay in. Each year I am faced with a student or two who assure me that they have done as much work as their friends and yet they are falling behind badly with their studies. In some cases I am perfectly well aware that the friends that they mention are working hard, even if they also go out and socialise enthusiastically. Be firm with yourself and those around you. If you have a study timetable to keep to, it is easier to stick with the studying and simply be unavailable on those nights (or during those lunchtimes or study breaks) when you need to get things done. You are not going to miss anything major by your absence, and you will be able to enjoy the social time that you do allow yourself.

One of the major advantages of establishing a firm social peer group at university is that when you have to find somewhere to live at some point in your degree course, it is much easier if you can share a house with friends. The benefit of spending some time in a hall of residence is that you can decide in advance of moving out who would be a good house mate in the future. You do not need the hassle of unpaid bills, a kitchen that you cannot get at for the mess or parties every night of the week; these can be a strain on even the best of friendships. Be honest with yourself: who amongst your friends would actually make the best house mate? Who is reliable enough to pay the rent with you, organised enough to keep the place reasonably tidy and dedicated enough to leave some nights free for study? The answer may not be your closest friend, but it will be someone with whom you can live without unnecessary distractions. If you begin to plan early, and team up with someone with whom you think it will work, you will increase your chances of getting a decent place to live, with someone who is not going to drive you mad by the third week of term.

Your course peer group

This group will become increasingly important within your degree management as your course develops. There will be members of this group who will also fall within your friendship groups, but there will be others with whom your relationship is much more of a trade-off. You work with them in seminars, or perhaps give joint presentations with them, and you will spend some time between lectures with them. The advantage of this group is that you immediately have something in common with everyone else: your course. You will be able to talk about problems with your studying, or confirm timetables and coursework schedules, in the knowledge that you will get reasonably reliable replies. You will also be able to gauge your progress by comparing your achievements with those of the other members of the group.

There are, however, potential disadvantages to this peer group. If you are finding things difficult, you may begin to feel that all the other members of the group are not pulling their weight, or are succeeding where you feel that you are not. Try not to let yourself be put off: it will not be the case that everyone is finding the course easier than you, or that they are all achieving better results in all the modules, so take what you hear with a pinch of salt.

You may also find that you work in a different way to other members of the group. If you work well in bursts and then take a break, your study timetable will reflect this. Do not let yourself be distracted by anyone else's work method; stick to your timetable, in the confidence that it will suit you. The same principle applies to revising. Some people find that talking about what they have learnt is the best way to revise, and they will organise discussion groups when the time for examinations draws near. If you are not in this category, resist the pressure to join one of these groups and continue to work in the way that suits you best. There is no harm in spending some time with your study group as you all revise, as long as you also spend time working through your own revision plan.

You can draw a lot of help from your course peer group when it comes to placements or events outside university. If you are undertaking a placement during a vacation, you might find that contact with the university is limited, so pairing up with another student on your course makes sense. You can check that you are doing the right thing, gathering the necessary information and producing the best results. Support such as this will not take the place of confirming the details with your department or tutor, but, if you can arrange to keep up regular contact with another member of your course, you can give each other moral support and practical help during any last-minute panics.

Within your placement, if you have one, as with all other aspects of contact with your course peer group, make sure that the trade-off works fairly. If you need to ask a colleague for the notes from a lecture that you have missed, be proactive in offering to return the favour. Equally, if you are working in a seminar group and have to give a joint paper or presentation, make it clear that you are willing to pull your weight. If you cannot make a series of meetings to discuss what you will all do, let the other members of the group know about your difficulty, offer to do whatever they think is fair, and make the effort, as soon as possible after each meeting, to find out what tasks you have been given, and do them within the time frame that has been set. Remember that group projects are usually given an overall group mark, regardless of the relative efforts put in by each member of the team. Your fellow students will be supportive of you and understanding about your other commitments, but this sympathy will soon evaporate if you get a reduced mark as a group because of your lack of input.

Your activities peer group
These peer groups develop as a result of your activities outside your course, such as your work in clubs and societies, or your involvement in your Student Union. Again, they may not include your greatest friends (although some overlap between all these groupings is likely) but they will help you to ex-

perience undergraduate life away from your course. They can provide a good escape from work, and talking with the group can be a real confidence boost if you are finding one aspect of your course particularly burdensome. This is especially true if you are working alongside other, more experienced under-graduates. They will also involve you in trying out new skills. You might get the chance to become involved in writing for a student newspaper or organ-ising student events. You might do some public speaking, or you may have to chair a series of meetings. These are all opportunities that are worth grasping: they give you the chance to try out your skills within a supportive situation, and they look good on your CV.

The only potential disadvantage to this peer group is that student societies are often run by enthusiasts, who are, as a result of this enthusiasm, happy to devote vast amounts of time to an organisation. This is fine, if you have the time, but remember that some students go to university with their degree as second on their list of priorities: their main aim is to embroil themselves in these other activities and have as good a time as possible away from the lecture theatres. If you are in a phase of your degree where your workload lightens, the demands of such a group will not be a problem, but make sure that you are very clear about what you can and cannot do. If you feel that you can devote one night a week to the organisation, then offer this amount of time and stick to it. Nobody will think any less of you because you restrict the time that you can give and you will be able to enjoy the activity without feeling that you are 'cheating' your studies. Being chairperson of the debat-ing society will impress any employer, but not if you also have to confess to having got a poor degree because you forgot along the way that you were meant to be studying.

Your study peer group

This differs from your course peer group, and is a much rarer and more valu-able group in which to be included. It will consist of only two or three of you, each of whom has found that you work well together, and can be of great benefit to each other. These groups will not form for everyone, and most students go through university without finding such a group, but if you do discover that you work particularly well with another student, who is on your wavelength and approaches study situations in the same way as you, or in a way that complements your efforts, it is worth nurturing the rela-tionship. Your study partner might not be studying the same subject as you: it is more about a way of working than the degree that you are taking. It could be, for example, that you can revise in absolute quiet for long periods at a time, but prefer to have some company whilst you do it, or that you enjoy talking through the framework of an assignment before you commit a plan to paper.

In both cases, having a study partner or couple who are studying a different subject from you can be a positive benefit. You will work quietly for a time and then take a break together, when you will either ignore the work you have done and give your brains a rest, or discuss what you have learnt, each of you talking about your own subject. If you are preparing for an assignment, you can discuss the plan in outline terms, even if your study partners have no direct experience of your subject. It is often the case that someone not concerned with your subject will ask the one fundamental question that you have failed to address, or will ask you to explain a point that you had assumed was self-explanatory. Again, you need to ensure that the trade-off works, and that everyone involved gets the chance to talk, but you will find that this grouping is amongst the most productive that you will make at university.

Your home support group
If you are a mature student, you will already be juggling your home and university life, but if you are a student living away from home for the first time, it is easy to forget to keep in touch with family, friends and colleagues from home. This might not seem to be a problem at first, but it can leave you feeling isolated when you leave university and, if you return to your home town when you graduate, you can find that you have few contacts left, which can be a disadvantage if you hope to network yourself into a career. Whether or not you are a mature student, and whether you are living at home or in a hall of residence, try to make the time to include your friends and family in what you are doing.

Keeping in contact with your home support group need not be a burden in terms of time or effort, and it will pay dividends throughout your course. If you have financial difficulties, for example, you will find the solution easier to find if your family is aware of what has been happening to you in the months leading up to the crisis. If you are a mature student with a partner, and perhaps children, you will be offered unqualified support in the early stages of your degree, but you will find this waning if you exclude them from your new life. You cannot assume that everyone understands what you are going through: you can get so caught up in university life that you fail to see how excluded other people feel; you forget that they might not understand how you are feeling, or they might feel confused about what you are actually doing. If you suspect that this is happening to you, take the time to make sure that you are including them in the experience: they will then be able to offer you constructive and realistic support.

As you can see, these peer groups overlap, and each has its place in your life as an undergraduate. However, each group can overwhelm the others, and not all peer groups are of equal value to you. You need to take control over your involvement with these groups: the secret is to recognise that they exist and use them wisely. Many of them will already be there for you, or will develop naturally without any great effort on your part, but peer groups can have a negative effect upon your chances of success, so treat them with a certain level of caution until you are sure that the trade-off is a fair one.

▶ Career placement opportunities

The greater emphasis being placed upon the employability of graduates is leading to an increasing number of opportunities for career and study placements of one sort or another at university. These may be called career placements, work placements or study placements. They may occur either within your university or elsewhere. You may not have come to university expecting this chance to be open to you, but then find yourself faced with the possibility of working for some period of your degree outside your university. If your degree involves a language, you will probably be expecting to study abroad, and this opportunity is also offered to Humanities and Social Science students who are not taking a language. If you are studying typography, your department may involve you in commercial work that might include your working with organisations outside university. If you are taking a vocational degree, up to a year of the course might be spent in commercial organisations. Even if your degree has nothing directly to do with commerce, you may have the chance to carry out a work placement. Inevitably, there are advantages and disadvantages to these placements, depending largely upon the way in which you work best, so it is worth considering them in some detail.

Some of the advantages of opting for one of these schemes are obvious, some are more subtle:

- The first advantage from your point of view is that the placement, however it is structured, should be very interesting. The lecturers and administrative staff who organise placements are highly committed to the concept of students working outside the university and make a great effort to ensure that the placements are relevant and interesting.
- Placements can make your course much more relevant to the career that you hope to pursue once you have gained your degree. If, for example, you are a typography or design student who has the opportunity to work on commercial projects, you will gain an accurate insight into how your degree work fits into the commercial world. A placement also allows you

to personalise your degree profile. If you are studying in a highly competitive field, such as management, the chance to include an impressive
work placement in your CV will give you an advantage over other graduates who have not taken up this opportunity. When you are interviewed
for a job, your placement is likely to be the aspect of your degree that
will be of most interest to your prospective employer.

- Placements can give you a feeling that a module can be finished off
earlier than other courses that began at the same time and this can
help you in planning your revision and coursework timetable. Short
placements are sometimes carried out over a vacation; this can leave
you feeling that you are ahead of the game when you begin your next
term's work.

- The placements that you are offered will usually be based upon sound
academic principles. They will not simply be work experience opportunities; you will be expected to analyse your activities and report upon them,
integrating the experience into other aspects of your course. However,
they can offer you valuable work experience. This may be your first
chance to work within a professional field, and having to appear at the
right place, at the right time and in the right frame of mind is both a challenge and a benefit. Undergraduates undergo a remarkably speedy and
profound change during their time on placement: they become more professional, feeling that their degree has a more defined purpose and they
have found the right career for them.

- More direct (and often unexpected) advantages can result from a career
placement. Employers get involved in offering undergraduates work
placements because they believe in the value of such schemes, but they
are also aware of the benefits to them of having the chance to see a
number of undergraduates in the workplace. They spend a fair amount
of time and money making sure that you get the best possible experience, and in return they hope to find undergraduates to whom they can
offer employment in the future. A number of students each year return
to university after a placement with a firm job offer; if you have enjoyed
the placement and it has confirmed your career choice, this is a great
boon for you.

- Some students find that working within a commercial organisation is a
welcome break from the demands of university, particularly if they want
to increase the transferable skills that they can offer a future employer.
If you feel that this might be the case for you, opting for a career placement will give you the chance to break up your study pattern and enjoy
a professional environment.

- If you are offered the chance to work abroad, either within a career placement or on a study placement, you will benefit from contact with another

university, in another culture and with work methods that might appeal to you. All that and, of course, the chance to travel.

The points discussed above may seem like an advertisement to send every undergraduate off on a career or study placement, but there are also disadvantages:

- You might feel that the career placements offered to you are not relevant enough to your degree profile to make it worth your while to opt for this choice. Before you reject the idea completely, however, make sure that you have explored the details thoroughly. You will probably be able to arrange your own placement, with the guidance and support of your department, and in this way you can make what might have been a wasted opportunity into a valuable aspect of your degree course.
- You could find that the placement schedule clashes with your timetable. Although departments try to ensure that placements are possible for each of their students, you might have opted for courses that clash with a placement, not necessarily in your scheduled timetable of lectures and seminars, but in the amount of work that you need to do in order to complete your coursework or revise for examinations. In these cases, a placement can be one burden too many and you will need to weigh up carefully the value of the placement and the stress of the resulting timetable.
- Practicalities will also have to be taken into account. You might be offered a choice of placements, all of which are some distance from your home or university. If you have to pay your own travel expenses, you might find these prohibitive. Similarly, if you need to go home for the vacations in order to earn money, you might find that devoting several weeks to a placement will leave you with financial difficulties to overcome.
- Placements involve you in working on your own initiative: you will have to liaise directly with an organisation, to ensure that you can fulfil their requirements, and it will be your responsibility to gain as much as possible from the experience. This may not be a problem for you, but if you feel that you might have difficulties in coping with what might be a situation unique in your experience, you will need to make sure that you have as much support as you need in order to be able to cope with the demands of a placement and benefit from the experience.

Managing a career or study placement involves many of the same principles as managing your degree as a whole. Although there is a great deal of variation between the career and study placements being offered in different universities, several rules of thumb will help to guide you:

- Find out everything that you can about your placement. You will not have to rely only upon the written information that you are given: talk to other students who have been on a placement already, and make sure that you know who is arranging the placements so that you can approach them with your list of questions.

- Even if a placement is a compulsory part of your course, avoid leaving it to the last minute to get hold of as many details about it as you can. Lecturers and departmental secretaries will be happy to talk to you about what is involved, but may be pressed for time if you leave your questions until the week before you have to commit yourself to one particular placement.

- Placements are often allocated on a 'first come, first served' basis, so make sure that you are one of the first on the list. Although the details of a selection of placements will probably be posted up on a notice board, there may be other placements available, and it is frustrating to find out, too late, that the perfect one for you has now been allocated to another student.

- Put your support network in place well before you begin the placement. In a lengthy placement (perhaps a year aboard or a 'sandwich year' in a course), there will already be an established structure in place. In shorter placements, you will still be allocated to a mentor and the staff at your university (particularly if you have a business liaison officer) will be on hand to help, but if the placement is carried out in a vacation, or if you are hesitant about contacting the university with what might seem to you to be a minor query, try to team up with another student whom you can call, even if just for a chat and some moral support during your time away from university.

- If you do have a problem, never be afraid to ask for help. Recent questions that I have been asked by students on their placements have included whether to wear a suit to work, whether they should address their mentors by their first names, whether they can use headed paper for their reports and who they should ask for time off to visit the dentist. These may seem like minor queries, but they are not minor if you are the one on the placement, and minor queries can easily become major headaches that prevent you from focusing on the task ahead of you. Similarly, if you are finding your placement disappointing, speak to your tutor whilst you are still on the placement. It is unlikely to be your fault, and your tutor will be able to improve the situation for you.

- Once you have arranged to go on the placement that suits you, and are clear about what is expected of you, make sure that you comply with the requirements of the placement exactly. This is, to some extent, simply a matter of common sense: there is no point in antagonising your mentor by arriving on the wrong day, or failing to take the right paperwork with you. It is also a matter of good time management: it is frustrating, and time consuming, for you to have to go back to an organisation asking for more statistics, or the company brochure, once you have left. If you have failed to carry out a task that you were set by your university, it will be impossible for you to make up the work once you have completed the placement.

A placement might become a vitally important part of your degree, even if you had not initially expected to be involved in such a scheme. The best way forward is to be absolutely sure about what is expected of you and make the most of all the support that is available to you. As with so much else at university, communication is the key.

▶ Successful student finances

By the time you arrive at university, you will probably have a financial plan of some sort in place, even if you still have the details to work out. You will know whether you will have to work to earn money and roughly how much you expect to have to raise in this way. If you are being funded or partially funded by your parents, your partner or other supporters, you will have had your fees paid and perhaps your hall of residence charges met before you begin. If you are intending to take out a student loan (a cheap form of credit compared to your credit cards), you will probably have arranged this before reaching university. Once you are at university, things may not go entirely according to plan, and there are books available to help you to budget, but the focus here is on how to make the most of the opportunities available to you, and some guidance as to how to avoid some of the common financial problems faced by undergraduates.

The successful management of your degree will rely in part upon your finances. If you are constantly worried about money, you will find it far harder to reach your study goals. There are some tips that can help to keep you within your financial schedule:

- Assess your financial position in some detail at the end of your second term at university. Students often overspend in their first term, and then scare themselves silly by assuming that they will be spending at this rate throughout their course. By the end of your second term, you will be able to get a much clearer idea of how your budgeting will work throughout the rest of your course.
- If you are being supported financially at university, make sure that you opt for as many fixed costs as possible. If, for example, your financial supporters know that your hall of residence bill covers your food and lodgings, they can feel confident that they have covered the basics. They

will then be willing to negotiate for additional payments if unexpected expenses arise. If you opt for a self-catering place, you will feel as if you are forever asking for cash for the basics, and this can leave everyone (you and your supporters) with a confused and distorted image of how much help you need.

- If you can arrange to open an account at the university's bookshop (or at a bookshop nearby if the one on your campus is not well stocked) with an agreement that your financial supporters will pay the bill as long as it includes primarily course materials, you will find that this reduces the strain on you considerably. If you are having to live within a restricted budget, it is tempting to ignore the need to buy books, and this can be a real hindrance to you, particularly when it comes to revising or working during the vacations. You could also buy most of your books second hand from your department. There are usually some bargains to be had, but undergraduates often find out about this only after they have purchased most of their books brand new.

- Find out as soon as you can how you can live within your means and still have a life. You will have your basic costs covered, and you may have some extra cash for socialising, but this will not go as far as you expected. Earning extra money is the obvious solution, but it is sometimes easier to reduce your socialising costs. Sometimes you can do both: if you want to meet more people, sitting in the Union bar all night is expensive, but working behind the bar will earn you some money and give you the chance to meet other students. You can also reduce your socialising costs by joining a club or society. This will give you the chance to spend time at meetings and other events with people who have similar interests to you without you having to buy drinks all night. Study nights, if you work well with other people around you, can be a cheap way of socialising. By designating certain nights as study nights, you have an excuse to invite around as many friends as you like for a study session. This is one of the cheapest nights about: no need for drinks, taxis or club entrance, and you might even get some studying done. It is worth finding out whether the events organised by your Student Union are better, and cheaper, than those offered in the local town. If they run a film theatre, for example, it will save you a lot in extra costs if you see films on campus; if they run club nights, you will at the very least save on a taxi fare, and will probably also find that the cost of entrance and drinks is cheaper.

- If you are in a social group where everyone seems to have more money than you, you will need to plan carefully. In essence, your approach will be no different to that outlined in the section on peer group pressure. Be clear about what you can and cannot afford and stick to it. You do not have to be the member of the group who is forever moaning about being broke, but you will have to decide how often you can afford to go out each week, and make the most of those nights, whilst considering some of the above options so as to improve your social life without stretching your budget too far. You will find that other members of your social group are in the same position as you (even if this is not clear at the outset) and so your restrictions on yourself will not make you a social outcast. I recently spoke to a student who had the opposite problem. His parents had made him an allowance of £24,000 per year just to cover his social costs at university. Interestingly, he felt like an outcast because he had so much money to spare: whatever your situation, it is best to be honest with yourself and then clear with your friends about how far your budget will go.

• If you suspect that you are going to be faced with unplanned costs, assess how this will affect your overall plans as soon as you can. You may, for example, decide to take up the option of a study or career placement, and this might involve you in travel or accommodation expenses that were not included in your original plan. This will be difficult to manage if you leave the financial planning until the last minute, but if you find out about what is involved early on, you can make arrangements in advance to cope with the additional expense.

Despite your best efforts, you might find that life at university is just more expensive than you, or your financial supporters, had expected. This need not be your fault and your supporters may be happy to cover the extra cost if, for example, you choose to study abroad, or if you want to join a society that involves buying equipment. If you begin to feel that things are going wrong for you financially, do not keep quiet about it. Financial supporters (particularly parents who might have had to budget fairly tightly themselves to send you to university) will be panic stricken if you arrive home with a huge and unexpected overdraft. If, on the other hand, you are able to work through the details of the situation before it becomes a crisis, you have a better chance of working out a solution. The first term will be expensive, but if you are still falling into debt by the end of your second term, you need to work out where, if anywhere, you can economise. If you have kept even a very basic record of your expenses, this will help you to work out the best way forward.

Students sometimes find that just one expense is distorting their plans, perhaps because they have to travel further to the campus than they had expected, their mobile phone bill shoots up horrendously or the reading lists for their courses are longer than they had anticipated. If you can show that there is one major problem, you are likely to be met with far more sympathy than if you are only able to give the vaguest idea of where things have gone wrong. Your financial supporters might be able and willing to help, in which case you will be relieved of the worry. If this is not possible, you will have to consider increasing your student loan (if you have not taken it up to the maximum limit already) or increasing your overdraft. Again, you need to involve your financial supporters sooner rather than later, they will be able to work out a revised plan with you and help you to apply for increased support. They will also help you to keep the costs of rescheduling your finances as low as possible. If your credit card is up to its limit, for example, it may be better for you to transfer the debt to a loan or overdraft.

For many students, the thought of increasing their loans, from whatever source, only serves to put them off the whole idea of being an undergraduate, and this is pressure that you could do without. If you know that you will be demotivated by having to increase your debts, it is a good idea to look into the possibility of earning some cash. You may already have planned to earn money whilst you are at university, or it may come as a nasty surprise when your budget fails to fit your lifestyle. In either case, try to avoid rushing into anything until you have checked your budget again thoroughly to make sure that you really do need to take this step. Having to earn money need not be a negative move: it can be a positive advantage if you handle the situation well and follow these guidelines:

- Firstly, make sure that you know exactly how much extra cash you need: it is not going to be easy for you if you take on work with set hours and then find that you need to switch jobs or take on an extra job in order to earn enough cash.
- Use the contacts that you have at university to work out what is available. So many students work to earn money that it is usually relatively easy to find out who the best employers are and what work is on offer.
- Make sure that you prioritise your personalised study timetable. This may seem like a luxury that you cannot afford when you are broke, but there is no value in abandoning your studying in order to earn money and you will be able to find work that suits your study needs. If you have a heavy workload at university each term, but relatively free vacations, try to make arrangements to increase your financial support in the term times, and then pay off your loans by working in the vacations. Similarly, if you work best at the weekends, try to earn money during the week, if your timetable allows you to do this. This seems obvious, but it is easy to panic and then forget that your study targets have to be met, despite your need to earn money.
- If you have to take a job, make sure that your tutors and lecturers know, if you feel that it will affect your performance. If you simply blame every disappointing grade that you receive on the fact that you have a part-

time job, you are unlikely to be met with much enthusiasm: after all, other students on your course will also be holding down jobs whilst they study. However, lecturers are realistic about this situation. If, for example, you want to change to another seminar group because it is held at a time that suits your work hours better, your tutor will be sympathetic, particularly if you can show that this move is part of your overall scheme of work.

- Universities are often desperate to find students who are prepared to work on campus. It may be that you are put off working in the Students' Union because you would rather not see your friends drinking coffee whilst you have to work, but there are other opportunities open to you. Libraries often need extra staff, departments need administrative support and Careers Advisory Services need help on open days and during careers fairs. These jobs may be short term, but that might be enough to help you over your financial problem, so they are worth considering.

- Students are often needed for less obvious work within the university. Psychology and Sociology departments will sometimes pay students to be involved in their experiments and these opportunities are not always widely advertised, so it is a good idea to make your own enquiries, perhaps by checking out their website or looking at their departmental notice boards. Acting as note-taker for a student with special educational needs can be both rewarding and lucrative work; it gives you the chance to listen to lectures and seminars in subjects other than your own and is a useful job to include on your CV.

- If you are looking for work beyond the university campus, you might decide to take a job in a fast-food restaurant or video store: these are always popular with students. These jobs have their benefits, of course. They can be well paid, the hours might suit your timetable and they are not likely to be too demanding of your brain power, which can be a relief if you are tired after a hectic bout of studying. If you decide to work in this type of job, be as creative in your search as you can: a late shift in a petrol station might leave you plenty of time for reading; sharing a job with a friend can give you flexibility as each of your study timetables become more or less demanding.

- You do not have to assume that, because you need to earn some cash, you have to take a job that has no relevance to your future career. Again, be creative in your approach and consider all your options. Call centres, dealing with customer enquiries and complaints, often pay well and the hours can be flexible. The work might be stressful, but it will look impressive on your CV. Administrative work may seem beyond your reach, but, if you have some IT skills, you might choose to work for one day a week in an office, perhaps with the option of increasing your hours over the vacations. Events and exhibition organisers often need extra staff for short-terms contracts. Again, the pay is usually good and the skills that you acquire will boost your CV. Market research tends to appeal to those students who are happy to talk to people in the street about their buying habits, and this work is usually available in bursts, which could be useful if you have a variable workload at university.

- You might expect that your Careers Advisory Service will only be of use to you when you are preparing to leave university, but in fact they are well aware of the need for students to earn during their studies, and they often advertise local jobs in their newsletters or on notice boards in their offices. Your earlier walks around the campus will have shown you where to look now and you will also find that the Careers Advisory Service is happy to help you to prepare a CV when you are looking for work.

- If you are hoping to work in your home town in the vacations, make sure that you do your research as early as possible and certainly during term time. Get the local papers sent to you, or ask your friends and family to look out for work opportunities for you. This will give you the chance to work as soon as the term ends and then take some well-earned rest, rather than spending the first three weeks of the summer vacation looking for work and then having no time to take a proper break before you return to university.

There was a time when students tried to live on their grants; then they tried to live on their loans; now many of them accept that they will have to earn some cash whilst they are studying, and they plan accordingly. However demanding your study schedule, it is possible to earn money without damaging your achievements at university. If you work to raise some cash, you will have a lower level of debt when you graduate, probably have cash to spare when you are at university and acquire marketable skills that will ease your transition into a career. The traditional image of undergraduates as continually broke but devoted to a student lifestyle is being replaced with the idea of students as financially astute participants in education, who can juggle their study plans with the need to earn money and who are, in a time of fierce competition, far more employable at the end of their courses. You will find that your finances are just one part of your life as an undergraduate: they need not hinder your progress, as long as you face up to problems as they arise and then work out, with help, the best way forward.

▶ Additional opportunities within university

During your time at university, most of your effort will be directed towards your degree course. However, universities offer a range of other opportunities and these are worth investigating. Each university differs in what it has to offer, but some of the more common opportunities are discussed below, to give you the chance to begin to think about what else you might do beyond your core studying.

University newspapers

It would be unusual if your university did not produce a selection of newspapers and newsletters, from the Students' Union newspaper, produced perhaps three or four times a term, to your department's, school's or faculty's student newsletter, produced perhaps just once a term. These publications offer you the chance to try out your writing skills. This opportunity is not restricted to those undergraduates who want to become journalists. It will look impressive on your CV, whatever career you are aiming for, and it could be one of your most interesting activities during your time at university. It is a form of studying, in that you will have to learn how to work to deadlines, within specified word counts and on an agreed subject, but there is usually a lot of leeway for students to pursue their own interests. If you pluck up the courage to present yourself at the newspaper's office, you will be welcomed with open arms. If you have an idea of the sort of subject about which you could write (such as music, politics, film reviews and so on), you will find this first step easier, but even if you have no more specific idea than just doing some writing, you will still be encouraged to get involved. If you are unsure about whether you want to write for the paper, there are plenty of other ways in which you can contribute: by working on the production of the paper, helping to design the layout or selling advertising space. All of these will give you new marketable skills to offer in the future.

Study skills courses

These are often specific courses aimed at helping students through particular areas of their study. Examination technique courses are increasingly in evidence, as are revision skill courses, courses designed to help you cope with stress and time management courses. These are in addition to the courses run by your Careers Advisory Service (such as CV preparation and interview technique courses) and they are usually run for a whole faculty or the entire university, rather than within a single school or department. They are not always advertised very widely, so you may need to explore your university's website to track them down and they are often heavily oversubscribed as the examinations draw near, so make sure that you find out about them early in your course and register as soon as you can.

Resource centres

All universities spend money on equipment that is held in resource centres, but these often seem to be well-kept secrets. Do not be put off by the lack of publicity: the equipment that you need will be available to you, somewhere within the university. If, for example, you have missed a film or documentary screening, a video machine and television will be available for you to use; if you need to interview subjects for a study but have no recording equipment, you can get hold of the equipment on loan. If you have to give a presentation using an overhead projector or a computerised data projector, you do not have to wait until the day of the presentation before you can try it out. If you need to use resources of this sort, contact your departmental secretary who will be able to point you in the right direction. The same applies if you need extra help in learning to use the equipment that will become part of your course: resource centres are usually staffed by highly experienced technicians who will guide you in using the equipment, so you need never feel at a loss.

Counselling

Student counselling services are always asking for more volunteers to man their telephone and drop-in centres. Although you will volunteer in the first instance because you want to help other students, this type of activity always looks good on your CV. You will also be offered training, much of it of a very high calibre, and if you are considering a career that involves counselling or communication skills, it is clearly of great benefit to you to have received some training before you graduate. Try not to let yourself be put off volunteering just because you have no experience of counselling: your fellow counsellors will have been in the same position, and you do not have to be an expert in all aspects of university life in order to help others in this way.

Working in schools and colleges

Universities sometimes work with local schools and colleges and their undergraduates might be involved in supporting children in the learning process in the classroom, or they may give presentations or drama performances in schools. Although your department may not be directly involved in work of this sort, your personal tutor should know if such a scheme is being run by the university, and by getting involved you will develop your teaching and communication skills.

Information technology courses

These have already been mentioned in Chapter 3, but it is worth repeating here that these courses are usually free for undergraduates. You can easily acquire several hundred pounds worth of training in a few weeks for nothing at all. You will probably attend an IT course (or several of them) in the early stages of your degree and perhaps when you are asked to do something new with IT, such as giving a presentation with a data projector. You will need to review your IT skills again when you begin to think about preparing a CV. Most careers will involve some IT, and the last year of your degree course is a good time to catch up with the skills that employers need.

Extracurricular courses

These are also called extramural courses and they are not always advertised in the standard university undergraduate prospectus. They are run alongside other courses in the university and are often taught by university staff. They usually cover areas that are peripheral to the university's degree courses, as well as some modules that can be used in accreditation towards a degree. They include leisure-based courses, such as local history or film criticism, and if you can get hold of a copy of the prospectus, you will have the chance to decide whether there are any courses that could underpin your degree or widen your ways of thinking and approaching your subjects.

Conferences

If you see a notice advertising an academic conference (or colloquium or research seminar) within your university or elsewhere, you will probably assume that it is for postgraduates or lecturers only, but this is not the case. If you learn about a conference that sounds interesting, see if there is a website where you can get further information. If you are nervous about going alone, get a friend to go with you by promising to return the favour in the future. Attending academic events such as these is an interesting experience in itself, and you can also expect to hear some as yet unpublished information and opinion about your subject from experts in the field.

Courses in other departments

Do not throw away your university prospectus once you arrive on campus; instead, take a look at it every term to see if there are any courses in other departments that might be of use to you. You might not have the time to go to a full course of lectures, but no lecturer is likely to object if you ask to sit in on one or two of the lectures that are most relevant to you. You might in this way be able to save yourself a lot of reading time with very little effort.

Languages

Language departments are well aware of the need to provide a variety of courses for students throughout the university. Your university's language departments might offer conversational courses, 'crammer' courses, beginners' written language courses and commercial language courses, yet it is not always made clear to students in other departments whether or not these courses are available to all undergraduates. If you are considering a career that might involve language skills, or are intending to study abroad during your time at university, approach the language department directly, through the departmental secretary, to find out what is available. The tuition will probably be free and it will be easier than attending a night school course.

Creative writing courses

Unsurprisingly, these are usually run by English departments, and are not always well publicised in other departments. You will never again have such an easy opportunity to polish your creative writing skills, and these courses will enhance your CV, so it is worth finding out about them during your first year.

Study trips

You will, of course, be given all the details of the study trips being planned by your department, but keep a look out for notices advertising trips in other departments. If you go to the departments of subjects in which you have an interest, you may find them advertising spare places on trips to the theatre, museums or events, or even trips abroad. Although these trips are designed with specific subject undergraduates in mind, places often have to be booked for more than the number of students available in order to get a good discount, and the department involved then has to hope that they can fill the spare places with other students. I once taught a student who waited until the cost of the foreign trips were heavily discounted in the last few weeks of booking and managed to get several enjoyable, cheap and informative holidays in this way.

Additional opportunities are, as you can see, plentiful at university but not always easy to find, so be persistent. You will have noticed that these opportunities can be useful for your undergraduate work, but are also helpful to you when you are moving into a career. Although this might not be something that you are concerned about during your first year at university, it will be a relief to know, in your final year, that as well as gaining a good degree you have been able to manage your time and opportunities so well that you are highly employable.

Spot guide

The key points to remember from this chapter:

- identify the peer groups in which you are involved and make the most of them
- make sure that the trade-off between you and members of your peer groups is fair
- try not to allow peer group pressure to have a negative impact on your studying
- keep in regular contact with your family, friends and colleagues outside university
- be clear about the amount of time you can devote to student organisations
- be open to the possibility of undertaking a career or study placement
- find our everything that you can about a placement before committing yourself
- have a support network in place before you go on a placement
- have a financial plan and review it after the first two terms at university
- include as many fixed costs in your budget as you can
- if you have financial problems, ask for help sooner rather than later
- if you have debts, make sure that they are as cost effective as possible
- when you look for job, be realistic about the amount of money that you need to earn
- if you take a job, try to work the hours and times that suit your study timetable
- be creative about the sort of paid work that you do
- remember to check out the earning opportunities on the university campus
- find paid work that boosts your CV as well as your income
- find out about the additional opportunities that are available on your campus and plan to sign up for at least one of them during your time at university

7 What if Things go Wrong?

Troubleshooting guide

Use this chapter for help in the following areas:

- if you are not sure how you will feel once you are at university
- if you lack confidence in what you are doing
- if you feel disappointed in the experience of being an under-graduate
- if you are finding life at university difficult, but are not sure why
- if you are having trouble coping with your reading lists
- if there never seems to be enough time to do what needs to be done
- if you have missed several meetings or seminars
- if you think that you might be taking the wrong course or module
- if you feel that you are being left behind your fellow students
- if you are often disappointed in your marks
- if you feel isolated
- if you are not sure how the personal tutor system works
- if you are finding your relationship with your personal tutor difficult
- if you are not sure where to go to get regular and constructive feedback
- if you have a specific problem that you can identify, but are not clear about how to get help and advice

► The emotional roller coaster of a degree

By reading this book you are taking an important and positive step towards ensuring that your degree programme goes smoothly. However, even with the minimum of hitches, you will discover that some aspects of your studying are easier than others and you will still find yourself undergoing a range of emotions, some of which may be unexpected. If you are to manage your degree effectively, you will need to be aware of these emotions and accept that they are normal: it is only in this way that you can be alert to problems as they arise.

Your feelings when first you arrive at university are likely to be fairly confused, as you would expect. You are being asked to fit into an entirely new environment, you may have left home to study and you are unsure of what is expected of you. This uncertainty is perhaps the biggest problem for all undergraduates: at many stages in your degree programme you will feel that, even if you are doing what you think is required of you, you cannot be sure and you are left wondering if you really are doing the right thing. Again, this book will help to reassure you that you are progressing as well as you need to be. You will also, at times, feel intensely lonely at university. This does not always hit undergraduates as they expect. You can fit into your hall of residence with no problems and find a new circle of friends quickly, yet you might still find yourself at some point feeling as if you are alone in facing a particular problem or that you are the only person ever to have felt this way. Again, this is a normal part of undergraduate life.

Feelings of insecurity are also normal, but they are none the less real for that. Insecurity can stem from a variety of sources, most of which will be explored in this chapter, but perhaps the greatest cause of anxiety is a creeping feeling that you have made a mistake coming to university, studying your chosen course. You may feel that you have chosen the wrong subject, you are not really clever enough to cope or you are simply not suited to university life. If a section of your study programme leaves you feeling inadequate or you are disillusioned with the course that you are taking, you might be reassured to know that this is a common experience. Beyond that, this chapter will help you to analyse what is going on and how you might tackle the problem. You might also be surprised to know that it is a feeling that is shared by even the brightest of students, so it is unlikely that you really are failing in any significant way.

Although your degree course will throw up all sorts of emotional responses from you, both good and bad, it is common to find that, once it is all over, you feel even worse than you ever did during the studying. This feeling of anticlimax once your degree is complete can be counteracted effectively in a variety of ways, and these will be discussed in Chapter 8, but at this stage it is the emotional path through the degree programme that is most important. Finding out what is going wrong, analysing why you feel bad about what you are doing, is the basis upon which you can improve your situation and this chapter will lead you through the emotional maze of a degree and show how you can overcome problems as they arise.

Essential dos and don'ts

Do:
- Read every notice on your department's notice board.
- Plan ahead, both financially and for your studying.
- Get help as soon as you feel that things are going wrong.
- Be firm with yourself: stick to your study timetable as well as you can.
- Ask questions if you are unsure about what is being required of you.
- Keep up contact with your department(s), just to make sure that you are not missing anything.
- Be clear about deadlines for assessed work.
- Keep in contact with your personal tutor: try never to miss your scheduled meetings.
- Get help with specific study skills when you need it.
- Create a support network that is appropriate to your needs and commitments.

Do not:
- Assume that everyone knows more about what they are doing than you do.
- Risk going ahead with a project until you are sure of what is required of you.
- Decide that you have to keep going with a course that you hate if you are in the early stages and can still make changes.
- Suffer in silence: there are many ways in which you can improve your situation.
- Keep going with a personalised study plan that is not working: make changes at the end of each period of study.
- Leave university early, or arrive back late, without informing your personal tutor.
- Ignore the opportunities that are available to you in terms of extra studying and preparing for your future career.
- Let down your team if you are producing a group presentation: you will probably need the support of your team members at a later date.
- Be inflexible about your study timetable: it is there to serve your purposes and can be altered as the need arises.
- Allow yourself to become so overworked that you stop thinking clearly about what it is that you are trying to achieve and how best to do it.

▶ The secret of discovering what is wrong

It would be far easier if you instinctively knew what was going wrong as soon as it began to happen; of course, it is more likely that you will feel a general sense of unease, a lack of motivation in your work and a waning of enthusiasm. Unchecked, this can develop into a sense of disillusionment with your whole course of study, even though there is probably only one aspect of your life as an undergraduate that is giving you trouble: the secret is to analyse what the problem is and then to fix it. The guide below will help you to work out what is going wrong for you and guide you towards the most effective forms of help. If you have a specific problem and know what is wrong (for example if you are dreading a seminar presentation or having trouble getting an essay in on time), you will find help in the previous chapters: this is intended as a summary guide for you to consult when you are feeling dissatisfied with your life as an undergraduate without really being sure why.

You seem to be spending all your time reading without conquering the reading lists

This usually happens in your first year, as you struggle to get to grips with huge reading lists, and it often affects the brightest and most enthusiastic students, those who feel that they must cover everything that is laid before them. Once you begin to feel overwhelmed by these lists, you will find that your reading becomes unfocused and you are reading more and more texts in a less and less productive way. You may also begin to feel that you are always behind with your studying. The first thing to do is to stop reading. Instead take the time to develop a realistic study programme that encompasses the amount of reading you can reasonably do. Decide what areas of study will require secondary reading and identify those where you can sensibly expect to do little more than read and understand the primary texts. Managing your degree means getting a balance between taking in information and giving it out. If you have to reduce your reading expectations to the bare minimum for a while, you will allow yourself the time to write essays and prepare for seminars, which will leave you feeling that at least you are covering the work required of you. There will always be time to do extra reading (perhaps as part of your vacation-study timetable) once you have completed the tasks that you have been set. Chapter 3 gave more detailed guidance on how to tackle this problem.

You are working for cash and studying and you continually feel tired

There is no denying that for most students the need to earn money leaves them with less time than they would like for studying and a heavy workload.

This feeling of perpetual tiredness tends to hit students in their second year and, if you have to earn some cash, it can feel as if you are trapped in a cycle of exhaustion. There may be no way to avoid this entirely, although Chapter 6 helped you to work out how best to earn money whilst you study. The solution to this problem lies in good planning. Make sure that you are working in the most effective way for you, either earning money in the week or at weekends, and adapt your study timetable to suit these circumstances. For example, if you have to work in the vacations, make sure that you cover as much as possible in the term time; if you are working in the evenings, try to ensure that you leave yourself enough study time at weekends to keep up. Most importantly, if you have to work longer hours for a limited period in order to earn money for a specific purpose (perhaps to pay off a credit card or pay for a holiday), be easy on yourself and reduce your study timetable to a minimum: with good planing, you will be able to catch up in the weeks to come.

Your coursework timetable leaves no time for extracurricular study or activities

Although this can happen at any time during your degree programme, it is most common in the second and third years. To some extent, it is unavoidable, as any degree course will involve fluctuating amounts of work as it progresses. It may not have looked like a problem when you were making your choices: it may not be that you have taken on more courses, instead it might be that you are being asked to undertake a wider variety of tasks. One of your courses may involve a placement, whilst another may require you to make a series of seminar presentations, with a third involving a heavy schedule of lectures. Chapter 5 guided you through choosing the best options for you, but if your workload seems to leave no time for you to tackle the reading lists or work out your own ideas, you can take comfort from the fact that this is a temporary problem. Your workload will change as you move on to new modules and you will find the time to keep up with the tasks that you have set for yourself in your study timetable. Again, planning is vital and you will need to dovetail your term-time and vacation-study timetables so as to ensure that you face your next modules without feeling that you have slipped behind.

You find that you are missing important meetings

This is a surprisingly common problem, particularly amongst students who are keen to cram as much into their time at university as possible. It can happen at any time, but particularly as examinations approach. Your first task is to decide whether you really are missing vital meetings. If they are revision sessions arranged by your fellow students, you will need to analyse whether they are essential for you. Perhaps you are already covering all your revision alone and so have no need for additional meetings. The group of students with whom you are giving a presentation or seminar paper may be arranging far too many meetings, perhaps because they feel insecure about what is being asked of them. If you are happy about your role in the task that has been set, and find that the meetings are just getting in the way of your studying, be firm with the group. Offer your support, be clear about your contribution and then explain that you cannot attend all the meetings but will do what is required of you. The advice in Chapter 6 helped you to do this in the most effective way. More serious is the feeling of panic that you get when you have missed one or two departmental or module meetings. You may not have been expecting to have a briefing meeting a term or two before a module is due to begin and you then panic when you realise that you have missed the meeting, and this can colour your whole view of the course; you feel that you have failed even before you have begun. There is some consolation in knowing that you will not be the only student to have missed the meeting (or series of meetings) and the only way to tackle this is to make contact with the tutor (or subject secretary) as soon as you realise your mistake. Although you will feel embarrassed, in reality it will not be a problem. It will be easy for you to get the information that you need and sign up for the seminars or lectures that suit you best. Missing these meetings is not an insurmountable problem, as long as you put the situation right at the first available opportunity.

You are beginning to hate your course

This feeling might arise in the first stages of your degree programme, but thankfully it is rare. Chapters 4 and 5 helped you to avoid this problem, but the main point to remember here is that an apparently 'wrong' choice is usually not that at all; it is simply that one aspect of a module is less appealing to you than others. This is easily resolvable: talk first to the lecturer who is running the course to find out whether it contains elements later on that will appeal to you more. If you still feel that your choice was the wrong one, speak to your departmental secretary to find out how feasible it is to change courses and then talk to your tutor about what you should do next. It may be that it is not the module that is the key to your dissatisfaction; perhaps you are experiencing other difficulties that can be resolved without the need to change courses. Do not be tempted to leave the situation without doing anything about it in the hope that things will get better by themselves. They probably will, but you need the reassurance now that your situation will improve.

You are not enjoying your life as an undergraduate

There are obviously a multitude of reasons why you might not be enjoying your time at university, and if you just feel vaguely unhappy about your situation, it is worth taking the trouble to consider what is actually going wrong. It may be that the problems listed here will help you to focus your thoughts, but if you are struggling to articulate the difficulty, even to your-self, try to take some time out from studying. Of course, you will not want to take too much time to do this, as getting behind with your studying will only exacerbate the situation, but if you can leave university for a weekend with the express purpose of assessing your circumstances, you will find that this is time well spent. Talking to friends and family can help: they often ask the questions that you would not have thought to formulate for yourself, and just being away from your university campus for a time can help.

Everyone else seems to be better informed than you

There are undergraduates who just seem to know everything there is to know about deadlines, seminar dates, examination timetables and so on; there are far more who spend much of their time anxiously assuming that they are missing out on vital meetings or writing essays with no clear idea of the deadline. It is comforting to know that it is often the brightest students who are the least organised, and this is a problem that can be overcome easily. It might be that you are not disorganised at all, but instead you are the type of person who becomes anxious over one missed deadline or meeting. If this is the case, or you are genuinely disorganised, the best way to cope is to find some more organised colleagues and stick to them like glue. By talking to them, you might discover a 'secret' source of information: maybe they talk to the departmental secretary regularly, use a journal that you are unaware of or have found a notice board that you have missed. Beyond this, you can create a useful trade-off, perhaps by getting your more organised friends to remind you where you should be and what you should be doing, in exchange for your involvement in a revision group or organising a specific group task. I once taught a student who was brilliant at all things academic, but who could not get through the day without meeting up with her more organised colleague each morning to check on what had to be done that day. When I quizzed her friend about this, she explained that it was no problem for her to organise her friend, as it came quite naturally to her to know what she was doing each day and she was happy to share her knowledge; in exchange her less organised friend had agreed to chair all their meetings when they prepared for seminar presentations, as she worked better under pressure and in group situations. The trade-off worked well for them both.

You are concerned that your degree will not get you a job

The final chapter of this book will help you to relate your degree course to the career of your choice, but it is worth bearing in mind that you are likely to need to keep the balance between academic activity and employability throughout your degree. A degree is an intellectual challenge and the pleasure of taking a degree lies in this challenge. You can also ensure that you are taking some courses that will make you attractive to employers, either in your main degree programme or in extra activities, but try not to worry about this too early in your course. As long as you have visited your Careers Advisory Service in the early months of your degree, you will be aware of the help that is on offer. You are increasingly likely to be asked to complete a career management module as part of your degree. Beyond this, try not to let thoughts of your future career distract you from the tasks that are immediately before you. Your university will be acutely aware of the need to make their graduates as employable as possible so, at least in the early stages of your degree, let them do the worrying for you. There will be ample opportunity during your course to prepare for your first career moves.

You are always disappointed with your marks

This might be a problem of unrealistic expectations, but it is much more likely to be a problem of communication. Although undergraduates are understandably wary of predicting the class of degree that they expect to get, you are the best judge of your abilities, and if you feel that you are underachieving, you need to get help. This will come in the form of tutorials and Chapter 5 has shown how essential these are, but if you are still left disheartened by your performance, there are other options. Firstly, talk to one of your seminar tutors (the one with whom you feel most at ease) to discuss the requirements of each course. Sometimes poor performance is caused by nothing more complicated than a student underestimating the range of reading that is needed, or the ways in which assessment is taking place. Your second port of call will be your personal tutor, who will be able to take an overview of your degree programme with you so as to highlight any areas of particular difficulty. Thirdly, if you have been able to pinpoint one area in which you have a weakness, do not assume that it will get better without any further help: sign up to a study skills course, reassess your study timetable or ask for additional guidance in that area. Lastly, do not get into a panic about just one or two disappointing marks, even if they are part of your assessed work. It can happen to any student: perhaps you have missed the point in one area of a module (this can be put right), you are just too overworked at the moment (this will ease) or you need to work harder in some areas and ease off in others (this will not be a problem).

You feel isolated

This can be a particularly acute problem for those students who are taking a joint degree or who are studying away from university for a time. Chapter 6 offered guidance about how to overcome this problem, but if you suspect that your isolation is more than just a practical outcome of your course choices, it is worth exploring more formal ways of becoming involved. Join a study group (this need not be confined to your subject area) or become involved in a student group that is not directly involved in your area of study. Arrange your accommodation so that you have other students around you, if this is possible, and spend as much time on campus as is feasible. If you find yourself isolated because your workload is too heavy, adjust your study timetable to include some nights off to allow yourself a social life: you can gain valuable support in this way, so it is not time wasted. You will also need to make the most of your seminar groups. You will meet with these fellow undergraduates on a regular basis, probably at least once a week, so they provide the ideal opportunity for you to create a support network. If the group meets outside seminars in order to prepare or revise, make sure that you are involved. If they do not meet regularly outside the appointed times, be the one to make the effort to arrange such meetings. You will find that other students are also happy to get support in this way, and study groups that arise from seminars can be especially useful when it comes to revising.

You feel low most of the time

There is an assumption that undergraduates will face a range of difficulties during their degrees, all of which are associated with studying, the need to earn money, the pressure to fit in socially and the challenge of passing exam-inations. It is true that these challenges exist for most students, but tutors and support staff (and students themselves) sometimes ignore the obvious. An undergraduate course of study is hard work: students are not all sitting around drinking coffee and doing little else. They work hard, sometimes under difficult circumstances, often earning money as well as studying and frequently trying to cope with their workloads with too little sleep and not enough time (or cash) to eat well and take some time out to rest. If you feel low for much of the time, finding it hard to focus on the work in front of you and feeling demoralised about what you are doing, check the sections above first to see if there is a problem that you can tackle head on and overcome.

If none of these categories seem to fit your circumstances, try to analyse how your overall living pattern is working out. Are you having to work more hours than you had anticipated in order to earn money? Are you getting enough sleep? Do you find yourself working, in one form or another, for too much of each day? Do you ever give yourself a complete weekend off? Do you continually feel that there is too much work and not enough time? Is your self-imposed schedule so hectic that there is no leeway for error? If you answer 'yes' to any of these questions, you need to sit back and take stock of your situation, working through the requirements of your course (and perhaps your job) and deciding how you can break up your pattern of work so that you can get enough sleep and rest and still achieve the desired results. Ploughing on through an impossible study timetable is going to be no help to anyone: you will lose heart and work much less productively. The point of a study timetable is that it acts as a monitor to what you are doing; it is intended to be flexible so as to allow you to do more or less work at different times and still produce your work on schedule. Do not be afraid to make amendments to your timetable and lifestyle if you feel that this is the problem. It is more common than is often supposed for undergraduates to be overworked, and if this is your situation, face up to it and make changes now, before you lose your way entirely. If, having taken these measures, you still feel low or tired for much of the time, do not hesitate to go to the university medical centre: that is what they are there for.

▶ Your personal tutor

The vast majority of students will be allocated a personal tutor for the whole of their time at university: this relationship will be a linchpin of your life as an undergraduate, so you need to understand how the system works and how to make the most of your personal tutor. The first, and most important, aspect of managing this relationship is to be clear about the level of contact that you might expect to have with your personal tutor, who will want to support you but who will also have many other tutees. You will be given the opportunity to meet on a formal basis, probably once or twice each term. A meeting at the beginning of term is an opportunity for you to discuss any concerns that you have about the courses that are coming up, and for you to alert your personal tutor to any problems that you feel might arise during the term. In most cases these meetings are just a formality, but make sure that you bring up any problems that you are aware of, as they will be easier to resolve if your tutor is clear about your situation and your concerns. A meeting at the end of term is essentially a 'mopping up' exercise, a chance for your tutor to make sure that you are aware of the challenges that you will face during the next term and an opportunity for you to discuss anything that has happened during the term about which you are still concerned.

The most important job that your tutor has is to support you between these meetings if things begin to go wrong. If you are unhappy with a course, unsure of how you are being assessed or have problems outside your course that are affecting your ability to study effectively, your personal tutor is well placed to help you. In order to make the most of the relationship in these circumstances you need to find out how best to maintain contact with your tutor. Some tutors prefer communication by email; some prefer to meet face to face; all will have a specific 'office hour' during which they are available for their tutees who just need to drop in for a few minutes to resolve a specific problem or arrange a meeting. Tutors are usually keen to help, but are left feeling frustrated if one of their tutees is underachieving and refuses to discuss the problem. It is perhaps a leap of faith to approach your personal tutor with a problem that is worrying you, but you will find that it is the best way forward. Remember that another function of your personal tutor's role is to provide you with a reference for job applications or research proposals, and this is made much easier (and you will get a better reference) if your tutor feels that he or she really knows you.

Two problems can beset the relationship between a tutor and a tutee. Firstly, you may be unsure of whether to approach your tutor if you find that you are not enjoying, or achieving as well as you had hoped in, a particular module or subject. The first person to approach, if you feel that you can under these circumstances, is the subject lecturer or tutor who is organising the module. This will give you the chance to explain your problem to the one person who is best placed to resolve it with you. Lecturers are enthusiastic advocates of their subject and will usually go to great lengths to resolve the problems of any of their students. If, having talked to the subject lecturer, you still feel at a loss, do not presume that there is nothing more that you can do. Speak to your personal tutor. In this way you can talk through the problems without feeling that you are being judged on your performance, and you can explore the options open to you in a much more relaxed and comprehensive way. Personal tutors are used to their tutees coming to them with problems such as this, so there is no need to feel that you are out on a limb; your personal tutor will be in a position to make constructive suggestions. You will be talking to someone who knows you and knows that you work well under most circumstances and you will get a sympathetic hearing and practical support.

The second, and much more serious, problem that you might have with the personal tutor system is if you find yourself allocated to a tutor with whom you simply do not get along. This is just a fact of life: it can happen, and is not necessarily your fault. It might be that you made a poor first impression, your personal tutor teaches a subject that you find unappealing or simply a clash of personalities. All these problems can be overcome. Your personal tutor will take a professional approach to the situation: if you failed to attend your first meeting he or she will not hold this against you for the rest of the course; if you do not perform well in his or her subject, this will not blind him or her to your good qualities. If the problem is one of personalities, even this can be overcome. If you take a professional approach to the situation, by doing what is required of you and demonstrating your willingness to work hard, your personal tutor will appreciate your efforts and respond to them. There are, naturally, occasions when a tutor and tutee do not hit it off. Personal tutors are not perfect, and so you need not assume that this is your fault, and there are ways around the situation. Firstly, you might find a seminar tutor with whom you feel more comfortable, and he or she will be able to help you with much of the support and guidance that you need. Your contact with your personal tutor will then be kept to a minimum. It is certainly possible to complete a degree course with very little contact with your personal tutor. The administrative staff will also be able to help you with the logistics of your course, and in this way they can cover some of the ground usually allocated to a personal tutor.

Rather than neglecting the problem by avoiding your tutor, you can try varying your approach. If you find talking to your tutor difficult, you might find that switching to email contact is beneficial to you both. The one thing that you must not do is miss meetings with your personal tutor. Once you do this, it is easy for your personal tutor to assume that you just do not care about your course, and it is very difficult for you to gain sympathy if you later want to make a complaint against your personal tutor. Of course, you will want to avoid the situation reaching the stage where you do feel the need to make a complaint. If you feel that your personal tutor is making your life difficult and offering you no support, it is best to tackle the problem constructively. Try not to jump to the conclusion that the situation is hopeless after only one or two meetings: give your personal tutor the chance to redeem the situation; everyone is entitled to a couple of bad days. However, if you believe that the relationship is not going to improve and you cannot find a way around the problem, talk to your departmental secretary or a lecturer whom you feel will listen to your problems. You will be placing the lecturer in a difficult situation, but he or she will be in a position to talk to your head of department to see if you can be assigned to another personal tutor. This is going to be a tricky situation for all concerned, but it is *your* degree, *your* one chance to get it right, so you have the right to get as much support and constructive advice as you can, and your personal tutor is an important factor in your success.

▶ Getting feedback

The need to get regular feedback during the whole course of your degree has been stressed throughout this book, particularly in Chapter 5 where seminars, tutorials and supervisions were discussed. The feedback will usually come to you from the academic staff, and as long as you make sure that you are crystal clear about what they are telling you, you will find that this feedback becomes an essential part of your learning process. However, your university will have a complex and comprehensive system of pastoral and practical support and care, and it is worth knowing what each part of the system is designed to do. Your university may not have all the services out-lined below in place, but some of them will be evident in every university:

- **University chaplaincy**: this is usually widely publicised and an active force in university life, offering both spiritual guidance, regular worship and pastoral support.
- **Administrative staff**: although the value of the administrative staff in your own department has already been stressed, remember that all the support staff within the university are there to help you, so make the most of their expertise.
- **Student counselling services**: most universities run a helpline for stu-dents, often running a telephone counselling service and a drop-in centre.
- **Student welfare officers**: based usually within your Students' Union, these staff are invaluable sources of information and advice.
- **Special needs support**: this is usually provided by a dedicated team of specialists who can provide help in areas as diverse as study skills work-shops and note-taking services for students with writing difficulties.
- **Specialist support groups**: usually run by students and not always well publicised, these groups are designed to serve the needs of specific groups such as mature or overseas students.
- **Medical centres**: you may automatically have been registered with a medical centre, but you do not have to wait until you are ill before you pay a visit. It is worth knowing where it is, and how it operates, before you need it, and these centres sometimes offer workshops in stress man-agement, which could be of great benefit to you as your workload increases.

These support services should be advertised in your student handbook, but they are usually mentioned in that part of the handbook that undergradu-ates skim over, as they may not seem relevant to you as you begin your course. Knowing that they exist is comforting, and your departmental or subject secretary will be able to point you towards them if the need arises. There is no need to feel hesitant about asking for help from these groups: their job is to help you and that is made easier if you ask for help sooner rather than later.

▶ Overcoming specific problems

So far, this chapter has considered general problems that could have a major effect upon the progress of your degree. Many students will go through their lives as undergraduates without any major problems at all, but they might still encounter occasional difficulties that are not disastrous in themselves, but can become so if they are ignored or handled badly. The secret is to know where to go to overcome these specific problems, and the guide below will help you to do this.

Problem	Suggested solution
You have missed giving a seminar presentation	Contact the seminar tutor as soon as possible: the seminar can probably be rescheduled
You have missed the deadline for an assessed piece of work	The penalties for this are harsh: every hour counts, so make contact to explain the situation immediately
You are ill during an examination	A specialist tutor in your department will deal with this: there will be forms to complete. Contact your departmental secretary to find out who can help, but get a doctor's certificate as soon as possible, as little can be done to help you without this
You encounter problems during a study or work placement	Have a support network in place, but talk to both your mentor in situ and your university tutor whilst you are still on the placement: do not leave it until you are back at university
You encounter harassment or prejudice of any sort	Do not suffer in silence. Talk to your personal tutor or make contact with the student welfare officer, who will be trained to deal with situations such as this
You have problems with your accommodation	Your university will run an accommodation office; the staff there will be able to help you, even if you did not rent your accommodation through them. Your student welfare officer will also be able to advise you

Continued

You are unable to meet your financial commitments	Family, friends, student counsellors and your welfare officers will be able to help, but remember that if you have a bank branch on your campus the staff there will be specially trained to help students. Do not give in to the temptation to remain silent: get help as soon as you need it
You are giving a group presentation or doing a a group project and one team member is uncooperative	Talk to the seminar or subject tutor: he or she will probably already be aware of the problem, but will be unable to take action unless you speak out
You have to leave university before the end of term, or will return after the beginning of term	Do not assume that nobody will notice: they will. Inform both your personal tutor, your seminar tutor and your departmental and subject secretary. It is unlikely to be a problem as long as everyone knows what is going on
You have lost or irreparably damaged a library book	This may seem like a minor problem, but it is not so minor if the book is worth a lot of money. If you have mislaid a book, renew the loan, explaining the problem. You can usually renew two or three times whilst you search for it. If it is damaged, discuss the problem with a librarian: you are unlikely to have to pay for a new book, as university libraries can provide professional bindery services
You have missed the opening seminars in a term	Go to the seminar tutor as soon as you realise that you have made this mistake: you can usually get copies of the notes that you have missed, or at least you will be able to make a note of what has been covered. This is a far better approach than just turning up and hoping that your absence will not have been noticed

Continued

You have not been accepted on a module of your choice	There is fierce competition for some popular modules if numbers are limited, but it is worth pushing yourself forward over this. If you have not been accepted, you can usually appeal against the decision, and you might also be placed on a waiting list
Your timetable clashes so badly that you are missing lectures and/or seminars	In the unlikely event that this happens to you, make sure that your departmental secretary knows as soon as possible. He or she is in the best position to make initial enquiries about adapting your timetable
You keep missing your mail	This might not seem like too worrying a problem, until you have a vital piece of mail that you miss. University mail trays for students are notoriously overfull with ancient pieces of mail addressed to students who never seem to have appeared. If you find this is a real problem and you are expecting an important piece of mail, such as a returned essay, you might ask the tutor concerned to leave the piece of mail in his or her in-tray for you to collect
You disagree with your marks	The tutorial or supervision should resolve this difficulty. If you have missed the tutorial and remain concerned, make an appointment with the marker as soon as possible. It is unlikely that any other tutor would be prepared to comment casually on another lecturer's marking, but if you are still confused after your tutorial, or you disagree with the marker's comments, particularly if it is an assessed piece of work, go to your personal tutor to discuss the problem

This chapter has covered the most common problems faced by under-graduates as they progress through university. If your problem is not included here, do not let yourself believe that your difficulty is unique, or impossible to resolve. It is neither of these things. Speak to a tutor or other member of staff with whom you feel comfortable as soon as you can. The support staff in your university are there to help you: and that is exactly what they want to do, as long as you will give them the chance to do it.

Spot guide

The key points to remember from this chapter:

- whatever you are feeling, and whatever problems you encounter, they are a normal part of student life, and the problems can be overcome
- the secret to solving your problems lies in identifying what is wrong
- make the most of your relationship with your personal tutor
- if you have a problem, there will always be ways in which you can get help
- if you begin to feel that things are not going well for you, get advice and support as soon as possible: you do not have to suffer in silence
- if you encounter a specific problem, be clear about what has gone wrong and follow the guidelines in this chapter to get help
- make full use of the wide range of support systems available to you whilst you are at university

8 Examinations and Postgraduate Options

▶ Coursework and examination timetabling

In Chapter 5 the discussion of module choices included the advice that you will need to be aware, at the outset, of the type of assessment that is involved in each of your course choices. This will not be a deciding factor in making choices, but it is useful to know whether you are likely to be panicking to finish coursework at the same time as trying to begin your revision, or whether the coursework can be completed some weeks (or even months) before you begin to revise. For some modules you might be facing both forms of assessment and this can have advantages, allowing you to shine in both coursework and examinations.

For those courses where examinations form part (or all) of the assessment, you will need to find out what type of examination is involved. This will be familiar territory from your previous studying, and getting past papers and checking the rubric (detailed instructions) for each examination will give you the information that you need. You might not be aware, however, that many universities now include past papers on their websites, tucked away somewhere, so find out whether this service is available for you. In some of your previous examinations you will have been allowed to take in some set texts ('open book' examinations) and you need to check with your department exactly what you can and cannot take into the examination room. Sometimes only one particular edition can be used and each text will be checked in the examination room. If you are allowed to take in texts, be careful about how you use them. It can seem like a gift to be given the chance to take a book in with you, but this should not tempt you to ignore the need to be thoroughly familiar with the text beforehand, including learning quotations if this is something that you find helpful. It is far too time consuming to plough through a book in the examination, desperately trying to find just the right quotation, so use this opportunity wisely. Anthologies of poetry or books of legal details may be allowed into examinations so that students do not have to learn vast tracts of the texts, and this can be helpful. However, you will need to adapt your revision technique so that, rather than learning a poem or the details of a law case off by heart, you learn the page numbers on which these are printed: do not be tempted to rely on time during the examination to look them up, they should be at your fingertips.

The issue of learning quotations in readiness for an examination often causes concern for undergraduates who are unsure whether this is a good idea or not. To some extent, you will be guided here by your usual forms of revision. If you know that you find learning quotations relatively easy, then you will continue to do this. If you have real difficulty in learning in this way, you will be more wary. As a rule of thumb, quotations tend to be more of a help than a hindrance. They prompt you in the examinations by reminding you exactly what it was you wanted to say, prove to the examiners that you know the text inside out and allow you to articulate succinctly the point that you are trying to make. If you have not learnt quotations before as part of your revision routine, it is a good idea to have a go at this now. It is enjoyable to feel that you have really nailed a text by being able to quote from it, and you might find that you have a hidden talent for remembering in this way.

Open and closed text examinations will probably be familiar to you; what might be less familiar is the idea of a 'seen' examination paper. These are rare, but they involve the paper for an examination being issued to students several weeks before the examination. The idea behind this type of paper is that students get the opportunity to work out what questions to answer, decide how to tackle each question and plan the answer in advance of the examination. Undergraduates then take the examination in the same way as normal, except that they have the answer, at least in planned form, in readiness in their minds. This can seem like a gift of an examination: in fact, it can be a nightmare unless you plan it perfectly. If you are taking a 'seen' examination, it is vital that you decide how to tackle it. If you write out and learn your answers in full, which may seem the obvious thing to do, you are then faced with the prospect of sitting in the examination room desperately trying to remember each word that you wrote and finding yourself floundering if you stray from your prepared script. The best way to manage this type of examination is probably to take a dual approach, if you have time. Decide on the right question for you, prepare a plan and then write out the essay in full. Then revise from the plan. Concentrate in your revision upon remembering the details of the plan (including any quotations) and just glance through your complete essay two or three times. In this way you will have a firm grip on your plan when you are in the examination, so you can write the essay without a problem, but you are not so tied to a form of words that you trip yourself up if you forget some of your complete essay. You will find that certain passages will come back to you as you write and you can include these, knowing that you will only have remembered in detail the finest of what you had previously written. In this way you get the best of both worlds.

▶ Revision timetabling

Examinations can be a reassuring part of a degree programme for many students. Although you will be nervous, once you begin to revise the ground will be familiar to you and you will relax into the process. For some students, of course, the idea of a revision timetable is alien: they may have sailed through their pre-university examinations without having had to do a great deal of structured revision, but at degree level this will be necessary. The key word here is 'structure'. As with other aspects of managing your degree, if you plan your time and resources efficiently, you will not waste time and effort on tasks that are unnecessary, and you will get a sense of how well you are doing. If you just meander through your revision without a plan, you will have no clear idea of what you have achieved so far and how much more work there is to be done. You are also far less likely to take proper breaks from revising and these will become as important as the work.

The first question that you will be asking yourself is how soon you should start revising. When degrees were reliant entirely upon 'finals', examinations at the very end of a three- or four-year course, the choice was easy: undergraduates began to revise several weeks or even months before the examinations, knowing that this was the final push towards their degree. Now that modular degrees are becoming the norm, students have to be more canny about revision timetables, otherwise they can end up feeling as if there is revision to do at every point of their degree course. Only you can decide how long you will need to set aside to revise for each examination, but there are some guidelines that can help you to get it right:

- Do not assume that you will need to allow the same amount of time for revising each course: those that also include coursework may need less time than those that are assessed solely by examination.
- Be confident about your existing knowledge base. If you have produced several seminar presentations during a course, or carried out an extensive project on one aspect of a module, you may know most of what is necessary already.
- Do not allow yourself to be sidetracked into going over old ground again and again: although it is a good idea to include some easier tasks in your revision timetable, most of the tasks should be relevant and necessary.
- Give yourself time to take regular breaks during each period of revision.
- Make sure that you include other tasks that you have to do (giving in an assessed essay, preparing a seminar paper) in your revision timetable.
- Allow yourself more time than you think is necessary: it is not a problem if you complete your revision early, but it is a nightmare if you end up feeling that you have not done enough work.
- Include a rest period of several days during your revision and at the end of the timetable: you need time to let your mind relax and contemplate what has been learnt.
- Build some flexibility into your plan: you will probably have to alter it as you go along; try not to panic if you have to make changes.
- If you are not sure about the amount of work you have included in your plan, check it with your personal tutor or fellow undergraduates, just to make sure that you are on the right track.
- When you have made your plan, put it to one side for a couple of days and then go back to it to make sure you have included everything and have given yourself a realistic amount of work to do in the time that is available to you.
- Try to vary the revision methods that you employ during your revision time.
- Despite the temptation, do not spend so long making your plan that you eat into your revision time.

Within these guidelines, you will want to make your own, personalised revision timetable, one that suits your needs and commitments; the revision timetable outlined below will give you some idea of how the overall structure might work. I have taken, for the purposes of this example, the student who appeared in earlier chapters. She is now facing examinations in a History and an English module; half the marks for English are assessed by coursework that has to be handed in four weeks before the examinations. She also has to give a presentation in Sociology and hand in an assessed piece of coursework in Sociology the week before the examinations; there is no Sociology examination. This scenario will not fit your circumstances, but it will show you the principles involved in preparing an effective revision timetable. The student has decided to begin revising eight weeks before the examinations:

Week One: Begin to work through English course notes, making revision cards
Finish preparing Sociology presentation
Prepare Sociology coursework
Attend examination technique study skills workshop

Week Two: Continue to work through English course notes, making revision cards
Begin to work through History course notes, making revision cards
Rehearse Sociology presentation
Continue to prepare Sociology coursework

Week Three: Finish working through English course notes, making revision cards
Continue to work through History course notes, making revision cards
Give Sociology seminar presentation
Prepare English assessed essay

Week Four: Final preparations for Sociology coursework
Write up English assessed essay
Finish working through History course notes, making revision cards

Week Five: Write up Sociology coursework
Hand in English assessed essay
Revise from History revision cards: plan essays

Attend group revision sessions for History
Revise from English revision cards: plan essays
Attend group revision sessions for English

Week Six: Overlap time for last-minute preparations for Sociology
coursework
Revise from English revision cards: plan essays
Revise from History revision cards: plan essays

Week Seven: Week off from revision
Hand in Sociology coursework

Week Eight: Review all revision cards
Make last-minute preparations for examinations

The details of this timetable require some explanation. Not all the techniques
that this student has chosen to employ will suit you, but they are all worth
bearing in mind.

Week One:
- The student feels that she needs some help in brushing up on her examination techniques, and so attends the study skills workshop before she
becomes too embroiled in revision.
- She has already done some work on the Sociology presentation, but in
finishing it now she is giving herself a variety of tasks to do, so that she
can work up to her revision more easily.
- This week is focused primarily on Sociology, but she is beginning to
prepare her work in English. She has decided to read through her notes
a couple of times, reducing the basic information to revision cards. These
will be small index cards, on which she will put the main points to
remember, including dates, names and quotations in coloured pen. In
this week she will be covering the ground that has already formed part
of her coursework, so the workload is fairly light: she already knows most
of this section of her course, and this revision session is more for reassurance than for anything else.

Week Two:
- Although Sociology continues to be part of her studying, she is now
at the easier stage of simply rehearsing her Sociology presentation and
continuing to prepare her coursework, much of which will have been
done in the preceding weeks. This work allows her some time off
from revision.

- She is now focused firmly on revising both English and History. The technique will be the same for both, although the heavier workload will be in History: she has more ground to cover here as the assessment is entirely by examination and she has to cover the whole course in detail in her revision.
- Having worked through the English notes that related to her coursework, just to make sure that she can use this information in the examinations if it is relevant, she is now working through that part of her English course that is assessed by examination. The technique remains the same, but the revision workload is likely to be heavier.

Week Three:
- The pressure is on to complete her initial English revision this week: this will take priority. She will be helped in this task by preparing the English assessed essay; this will keep her focus on English, and it should be fairly easy to write as she did the preparatory work in week one.
- History revision will continue and she must be careful not to neglect this work even though she will be anxious about her seminar presentation in Sociology.
- Giving a Sociology presentation here is useful: it will add variety to the workload.

Week Four:
- By remaining on track with her History revision, she will give herself the chance to spend some time just working through her notes, in contrast to the other tasks of the week.
- Completing the preparations for the Sociology coursework should be a relatively easy task: much of the preparation work was done in weeks one and two, and a week away from the material will have helped to improve her focus on what still needs to be done. This will (hopefully) be very little, and she will be ready to write it up without too many problems.
- The English assessed essay should also be ready to write up and this will allow her the opportunity to balance her tasks between reading, revising, preparing and writing.

Week Five:
- The balance that she is trying to achieve between different tasks continues this week, with work to be handed in and revision to be continued. Last-minute work on her Sociology and English assessed coursework might distract her a little, but by now she has worked through

all her course notes for History and English, so the rhythm of her revision will change and this will keep her enthusiastic about the tasks before her.

- Reading through revision cards is not the most inspiring work and she has decided to attend some of the revision sessions organised by her seminar groups. She has left this until now because she did not want to feel intimidated by facing a group of students who might all seem to know more than her. At this stage she can feel confident that, having worked through all her History and English course notes, she has a good grasp of the relevant information. This strategy of meeting with other students to revise will only succeed if it suits her ways of working, and she may decide to do more of these sessions or continue to revise alone. If she does attend more sessions, she will need to ensure that she does not neglect her other revision strategies, such as reading through her cards on a regular basis and planning essays.

- Revision does not work well if it is a passive process. The student has avoided this by making revision cards as she read through the course notes for English and History. By obtaining copies of past examination papers, she is able to continue to be an active participant in the revision process. She will not have time to write out practice essays in full, but she will be able to work through past examination questions and plan her answers. This will help her to revise the facts that she has already learnt and assess how well she is doing.

- There are several areas in History that she hardly worked on at all when she was working through her course notes, as she is fairly certain that she knows the material very well already. By working on some essay plans in these areas, she can decide whether this was the best strategy or whether she needs to do some more detailed revision on them.

Week Six:
- This is a good opportunity to add any finishing touches to her Sociology coursework. Most of the work will be covered by now, but if any more work needs to be done she will not panic as she does not have to hand it in until the following week.

- Her objective in English and History this week will be to avoid boredom. The revision will need to be varied between planning essays, reading through her revision cards, meeting with other students and checking that every area of each subject has been covered. All these approaches might be useful, although she will have to resist the temptation to spend hours chatting about the work to her fellow students, to the detriment of some concentrated revision time.

- She will need to be confident about her abilities at this stage: if she knows one area of a subject, she must avoid going over it again and again, as this is guaranteed to demotivate her. Instead, she must focus on those areas where she is less sure of herself.

Week Seven:
- Surprisingly, students often find this the most difficult week to cope with. Once she has handed in her Sociology coursework, she must try to do very little revision. There is, of course, no point in getting stressed out because she is worrying about not working at all, but the less work she can do this week the better, as long as she is up to date with her revision plan.
- Inevitably, revision timetables do not always go according to plan, and this week can be a life saver if it allows her to catch up if she is behind, but it is far better for her to do nothing and just allow the information to settle in her brain. She will return to revision the following week feeling less exhausted and in a far better position to judge what last-minute preparations need to be done.
- This week will also be the perfect opportunity to get to grips with the details of the examinations: Is she sure that she has the times right? Does she know where each examination is to be held? Is she clear about the format for each examination? By making sure that she is certain about the practicalities of the examinations now, she will avoid last-minute panics next week.

Week Eight:
- By now, she will know everything that she is ever likely to know about the subject in which she is going to be examined, so why revise any further? The answer is threefold. Firstly, she can boost her confidence by going through her revision cards and reminding herself of what she knows. Secondly, she will be able to brush up on those few facts that are never going to lodge permanently in her brain (difficult names, dates and quotations, for example) and that she will be still be staring at in the minutes before the examination. Thirdly, she will need something to do. In the first weeks of this revision timetable she will have had to force herself to do anything; by now she will not be able to sit still, and by working through the cards, even if some of the time her mind is blank, she will allay her nerves.
- The last-minute preparations for the examinations are often practical things, such as making sure that everyone knows when you are taking the examinations, arranging a lift to the examination rooms if they are some distance away, shopping for instant meals and getting some sleep.

There are also some last-minute revision tasks that she might need to do. If by now she has realised that there are some facts that she just cannot remember (and this happens to us all), now is the time to make a series of revision cards (no more than two or three per examination) that just contain lists of facts, names and quotations, so that she has something constructive to glance at in the minutes leading up to the examination.

▶ Revision and examination technique

The revision timetable given here will show you how you might fit your revision into a specified period of time. You may decide to take more or less time to revise, but you will benefit from making a plan of some sort, and also by varying your revision techniques as your revision progresses: there is nothing like boredom to kill your enthusiasm. Whatever your plan looks like, there are some techniques that you can usefully employ:

- Remember that you must revise in the best way for you. You will know already whether you work best with other people or alone, but you will also need to think about the time that you spend revising. If you work well in short bursts of activity, with plenty of breaks, do not pressurise yourself into thinking that, because you are working at degree level, you must change your routine to include hours and hours of uninterrupted revision. Some people cope well with this approach, but most students need to take breaks fairly regularly if they are to keep going.
- If you are unsure about how long to work at a stretch, try monitoring your work rate as you progress. If you manage to reduce ten pages of notes into revision cards in the first half hour, and then find that you have only managed to get through half that amount in the next hour, check first whether the later course notes are more complex. If they are not, then an hour is about the time that you can spend working before you take a break.
- Make sure that your breaks are structured: you will find that you need very little distraction before you are ready to work again, so aim to treat yourself with a bar of chocolate or a short walk after a set period of time, but then go back to the revision. It is far better to take several short breaks during the morning than to take one long break that disrupts your train of thought altogether.
- Remember that time spent away from formal revision can still be productive time. You will soon find that you are mulling over examination questions in the shower, and talking about academic theories to your

friends over pizza, and this is all to the good. You may have some days when you actually sit down and revise very little, but during which you take several opportunities to work through the revision in your mind. As with other aspects of managing your revision, it is a case of getting the balance right.

- Accept that some days are just bad revision days. If you find yourself yearning to put on the washing, aching to clean out the fridge and drowning in cups of tea, you may have to accept that today is not the day to work on your revision. This can be scary, as you will feel that every day should be crammed with revising, but you must trust your instinct on this. If you make yourself leave it alone (and, for much of the revision timetable given here, there were other things that the student could usefully be doing), you will come back later (perhaps the next day) in a much more productive frame of mind. Your revision timetable will keep you on track, and being flexible in your approach is a vital aspect of successful revision.

- It is very satisfying to do some revision on material that you already know quite well: for at least one of the sessions above our student was likely to feel that she knew the salient facts already. If you find yourself in this position, enjoy it. You can tick off a session of revision having had an easy time of it. There is no need to worry that you are not working hard enough: there will be plenty more difficult sessions ahead.

All undergraduates will have had some experience of examinations, although if you are a mature student this may have been some time ago. You will know how well you perform in examinations and, if you are aware that you have problems with them, you can take steps to alleviate the situation, perhaps by choosing more coursework assessed modules, attending study skills workshops or practising on past papers under mock examination conditions. There are books available to help you with your examination technique if you feel that the examinations are going to give you real problems. For most undergraduates the points below will be enough to serve as a reminder of how to achieve at your best:

- Make sure that you are absolutely clear about every practical detail of the examination that you are to take: there is no point in wasting your energy on panicking about where you should be and when you should be there.
- Try to eat well and get plenty of sleep during the examinations, but do not panic if you cannot sleep. Examinations are largely undertaken on adrenaline, and even if you hardly sleep at all during the examination period, this is unlikely to impair your performance much. Remember that

rest is what you need. If you have trouble sleeping, watching a film is a good way of switching off and giving your body and mind the rest that they need: it is better than laying awake fretting for hours each night.

- Have confidence in yourself. You are at university because you have been judged capable of the work, you have worked hard for months for this examination and you will perform well, however unlikely this seems in the hours leading up to the examination.

- If you are anxious that you will forget a set of facts or figures during the examination, write them on one of your revision cards and read this just before you go into the examination and then, as soon as you begin, write them on your planning sheet of paper. You might never use them, but at least by getting them down on paper they are out of your head, safely stored away, and you will not waste your energy in the examination on pointlessly worrying about them.

- Whilst you are waiting for the examination to begin, try a few relaxation techniques before you do anything else. Take a couple of deep breaths and let them out slowly. Lower your shoulders (you will probably find that they are up around your ears at this point) and open your hands, as they are probably bunched into a fist by now. Also try to relax your tongue. This may sound strange, but your tongue is a big muscle, and by relaxing it (it will by now be stuck to the roof of your mouth without you realising it) you will relax your whole upper body.

- Write your name and examination number (this will stop your hands seizing up with nerves) and then read the instructions and questions, making sure that you understand them fully. Then read them again (you may have missed something vital in the first read through). Decide what questions to answer and in what order you want to answer them: usually the best questions first and the one that you are least sure about last. Before you get confused, do a rough plan of your first answer. This will include the five or six main points that you want to make, backed up by any facts and figures that instantly come to mind. Once you have done this basic plan, read through the question again: Are you sure that you have understood it and covered all the points that they are asking for?

- Take another deep breath at this stage and go back to the basic plan for your first answer, fleshing it out with all the more subtle points that you want to make. You may need to alter the overall structure: perhaps one point has become two, or two points could usefully be made into one. Decide now on the best ordering of your points and try to think of how you might link them. This process will be repeated for each answer as the examination progresses.

- You will know in advance how much time you can spend on each answer, so check now on your finish time for the first answer (leaving time for checking) and begin to write. At various points during your writing (usually every ten minutes or so) make sure that you are on track for time. Roughly speaking, if you have three hours to complete three questions, you will spend 10 minutes planning each answer, 45 minutes writing the answer and 5 minutes checking the answer.

- Make sure that you do check your work, both as you write, by glancing back at the question to make sure that you have not missed anything, and at the end. This last check is the one most often left out by students, but it is an essential part of your examination performance. You may not have the time to make major alterations, but you will be able to correct the name that you got wrong, or include the dates that you left blank because you could not remember them as you wrote: all those things that make you cringe as you reread your work.

- If you are running out of time as you write, leave a space large enough to insert a note directing the marker to the end of your script in case you get time at the end to go back and add some more information. This is particularly useful if there is an area that is not central to the point that you are trying to make, but that you would like to include if you get the time.

- Resist the temptation to run too far over the time that you have allowed yourself in order to complete an essay. Once you have left space to come back to a point (or several points) if you get time later on, continue with the answer and make your strong closing statement, then move resolutely on to the next question. It is easier to pick up marks by completing all the answers than to try to get top marks on the first answer but then complete only half the last answer.

- Even if you are told that the markers will not directly mark your plan, make sure that it is both legible and detailed. A line crossed through it will make it clear to the marker that it is not part of your answer, but if you run out of time your plan will at least give the marker the chance to see what you might have done and so assess your overall level of knowledge and ability.

- If you need anything in the examination, do not sit in silence, wasting valuable time. If you need a glass of water, ask for one. If you are unsure about the instructions, ask for help. The invigilators will tell you if they are unable to answer your queries and they will certainly be happy to help if they can, get you water, give you more paper and so on.

- Do not view the marker as a monster. If you want to say something but cannot for the moment remember the technical term for a process, or the name of a character in a book, it is better to describe the process or the character, explaining if necessary that you have temporarily forgotten the correct term or the character's name, rather than simply avoiding mentioning the process or the character at all. You will of course avoid anything like an appeal to the marker for a better mark, but markers are used to seeing notes in examination scripts and so will not be fazed by it.

- You will need to decide which is the best strategy for you in terms of planning and checking. Some students like to make very detailed plans, reasoning that, once the plan is written, they can relax and focus on making their writing as effective as possible. Some students find that a fairly basic plan will do. In either case, you will need to do a plan of some sort. Some students prefer to check all their examination script at the end, whilst others find it calming to review each answer as they complete it, before moving on to the next question. Again, adopt the strategy that suits you best, as long as you leave some time for planning and checking. Although the temptation to write madly until the very end of the time allowed is great, you can lose so many marks by making basic errors (errors that you would never make under less pressurised circumstances) that you are unlikely to be able to make up this ground, however much you write, so checking, even the most cursory sort, is vital.

- Once you have completed the examination, forget about it. Although there is always a group of students anxiously hanging around outside the examination room, comparing notes on every sentence that they wrote, this tends to be counterproductive in most cases. If you are genuinely concerned that you have entirely missed the point of a question, then there is some value in checking this with one or two of your colleagues, always remembering that they might have misread what was expected of them. Other than this brief check, try to move straight on to your next task. You have done your best, there is nothing that you can do to change it and you now need to focus upon the next examination.

If you are unfamiliar with the idea of making a plan for each examination answer that you give, you might find the outline plan below a useful guide to how you might go about preparing your own plans when the time comes. The examination essay will be based upon the lecture example used in Chapter 5. The student has an hour to complete the answer, and will spend 10 minutes producing this plan, with the intention of writing the answer for 45 minutes and then checking for the final 5 minutes. The question on the examination paper is 'Can John Donne's "Song" be taken as a true expression of the poet's feelings, or is it a more distanced analysis of love and separation?'

Initial draft plan (3 minutes to prepare)
Donne – 1572–1631 Wife's name was Ann More
Remember to refer to the speaker, not the poet

1. Courtly love poetry – not necessarily personal
2. Manuscript circulation, so might be used by several people
3. Donne travelled, so might have been written at a time of separation
4. Romantic language – personal? Talk about the language generally
5. Clever imagery – not personal? Not immediate?
6. Religious poetry – refer to it somewhere
7. Refer somewhere to Marvell's poetry – also seems personal but might not be

As you can see, the student has begun by jotting down points that she might forget, such as Donne's dates and his wife's name, and ideas that will act as triggers for the development of her ideas. She has also reminded herself to refer to the speaker in the poem, rather than the poet, as she knows that she has problems remembering to do this.

She now takes another deep breath and checks back to the question. She decides that she is covering the right ground in this first plan, but also realises that she can compare Donne's work to the poetry of the Romantic poets (the word 'romantic' in her plan probably jogged her memory) and will include this in her more detailed plan. Upon reflection, she decides that points 1 and 2 could be joined to form one first, strong point. She includes possible opening, connecting and closing sentences in her detailed plan as they come to her mind. She also decides that the order is not quite right.

More detailed plan (7 minutes to prepare)
On first reading this poem, one might be tempted to see it as an intensely personal poetic response to an imminent separation between the speaker and his lover:

1. Details of Donne, his wife and his travels
2. Language – romantic and lyrical (do some detailed analysis of the language of the poem), but not as immediate and simple as the language of some romantic poets (give examples)

Continued

3. We know that Donne worked through his emotions in his religious poetry (give examples in detail if time), but this does not necessarily mean that this is a purely personal poem

The poetic tradition within which Donne was writing would tend to argue against the reader viewing this poem as no more than the genuine and immediate expression of the poet's individual feelings:

4. Courtly love tradition and manuscript circulation (give other examples) tend to argue for a more distanced relationship between the poet and his work
5. Compare to Marvell's poem 'To his Coy Mistress' which is another example of a metaphysical poem
6. Finish on a discussion of metaphysical poetry and the concept of a metaphysical conceit, with examples if time

Although the reader's response to this poem might lead one to hope that the work is the result of highly personal and heightened feelings generated by the possibility of separation, it is impossible to ignore the genre within which Donne was producing his poetry and the evidence of the work of other metaphysical poets. In retrospect, the poem must be viewed as an engaging and intellectually challenging piece of writing that remains moving regardless of whether it was intended as a metaphysical analysis of love and separation, articulated by an abstract speaker, or a private poem to be exchanged between the poet and his lover.

In the examination, the student might make a more detailed plan than this, perhaps by including the titles of other poems to which she will refer, or quotations that she wishes to include. She might also make a note of how she will link her paragraphs, if she knows that this does not come naturally to her. She has given herself some flexibility here, deciding to give details of Donne's religious poetry and the work of other metaphysical poets only if she has the time to do so. She has not remembered everything from the lecture, but she has recalled enough to write the essay, and she will probably remember more details as she begins to write.

When she has completed the detailed plan, she will be acutely aware that ten minutes of her time for this answer has already passed. She will now be eager to begin writing, after a final quick glance back at the question to make sure that she has not missed anything. As this will be at least her third check of the question, she can be sure that she has got it right, and this is one less thing for her to worry about when she leaves the examination room. Now that her plan is safely written down, she can relax a little and concentrate on articulating her thoughts as well as possible, focusing on the best use of language. These are niceties that tend to get forgotten if you do not have a plan. She can complete her answer knowing that the most difficult part is over. At the end of the paper she will have time to check over the whole examination script, and so can leave the examination knowing that she has not let herself down in any way.

Managing the examinations that will form part of your degree is principally about planning: planning your revision timetable, planning to use your time effectively, planning to utilise a variety of revision techniques and, finally, planning your examination answers. If the planning is right, the tasks before you will be much easier.

▶ How to cope with the post-examination anticlimax

When you are revising, you will spend some of your time daydreaming about what life will be like after examinations. You think about the freedom to do nothing all day and the pleasure of reclaiming your life. Then, when you wake up the day after the last examination, you may be surprised by a feeling of anticlimax. You have spent weeks working in a very structured way and it can be difficult to cope with the unexpected sense of loss, although it is quite normal to feel this way. The way to cope with this is to have plenty to do in the days following the examinations. You will already have planned to catch up on your sleep and your socialising, but try also to arrange to do some studying at this time. Universities are aware of the deadening effect of the post-examination anticlimax and will usually get you back to work relatively swiftly.

This sense of anticlimax is heightened when you finish your degree course in its entirety. Although this is normal, it is often unexpected, and you need to find an antidote. For most graduates, the answer is to move as quickly as possible onto the next stage of life, although you will need to make sure that you do not make snap decisions about what to do next. It may be that you already have a job lined up, in which case make sure that you have arranged a starting date that is a few weeks after you graduate, if you can, so that you can get some rest. If you are intending to spend some time looking around for the best job with which to begin your career, you may need to decide whether to remain near your university for the summer or return home. Your instinct will probably be to return home, but it is worth considering spending at least a few weeks doing a temporary job in your university town. After all, you know the area and the job market there, your friends may be staying on to take up their new jobs and you may feel less isolated by remaining than by going home in these early stages. You will know what is the best choice for you, but it is a good idea at least to consider staying in your university area for a while.

▶ Postgraduate possibilities

Managing the first few months after you graduate is an integral part of managing your degree well. You are doing your degree for a purpose beyond the sense of achievement that it will give you: you also hope to get a job or go on to further research or training. The final chapter of this book will deal with the challenges of getting a job, but you might also be considering other options and these will be explored here. If you know what you want to do in life, your options at this stage may already be decided for you. If, for example, you intend to become a teacher, you will move on to a postgraduate Certificate in Education as soon as you have graduated. For many Humanities and Social Science graduates, a level of additional training is necessary before you move into your career. This may take place whilst you work, but you might have to complete a stand-alone course before you can enter your chosen career. Again, this is relatively simple for most graduates who know where they want to be in the long run: they will already know about the training courses that are available and will have applied to them during their last year at university. This is one of the most useful services provided by your Careers Advisory Service on campus: they will be able to guide you towards the best training course and help you to apply for it. What many graduates do not realise is that their Careers Advisory Service is still available for them once they have graduated: you can go back to them in the future to get further help and advice, so you need not feel isolated once you graduate.

If you are not sure exactly what career to choose when you graduate, you will not be alone: this will be the case for many Humanities and Social Science graduates, and you need to have a strategy in place to help you to move forward. The first year or so after you graduate is not going to be vital to your long-term CV: if you spend this time moving from job to job, it will not stand against you once you have decided upon a career; indeed, employers often look upon this favourably, appreciating that you have taken the time to come to the right career decision. You will probably need to earn money, but this can be achieved in a series of temporary jobs that allow you to try out different careers or whilst travelling abroad. You might also be in a position to arrange a series of career placements during this time. As long as you can afford to do it, it is worth considering spending some time in the first year after graduation shadowing a professional who is working in an area that appeals to you, or working on a voluntary basis for an organisation that interests you. This is a time to hold your nerve: you might feel pressure to get a 'real' job right away, or suspect that this type of work is going to get you nowhere, but in fact you can save yourself a lot of time in the future by working out what you want to do in these early stages of your career, and undertaking career placements can be the ideal way to do this.

Arranging your own placement when you have graduated, even if it is only for a couple of weeks in the summer, is a great way to show yourself off to a prospective employer. In highly competitive fields it is relatively common for graduates to approach their career in this way. Be prepared to make a direct approach to an organisation and accept that you might be working for a nominal fee. What you will gain from such a placement will make it worth your while, even if you are not earning a realistic salary for a while. There are four points to remember in managing this aspect of your graduate career:

1.   Make sure that you remain open to all the possibilities: do not assume that just because an organisation has no vacancies that it will be unwilling to take you on a placement.
2.   Remember that you will be on trial throughout your placement: see it as a way for you to find out if this is the career for you, but also as an extended interview, during which the employer will be judging how well you fit into the organisation, perhaps with a view to offering you a place on a graduate recruitment programme.
3.   Be prepared to do the research yourself: you will need to find out about likely organisations, to make the approach yourself and be flexible about what you are prepared to do.
4.   Use your Careers Advisory Service: they can help you to investigate an organisation and present yourself in the most favourable light.

Most students feel that, once they have graduated, they never want to study again. This is a temporary feeling and it will pass, but for some the degree is not enough and they want to continue with further research, usually by undertaking an MA or a PhD. You might not consider this option until the last minute and this can be a nuisance. You will need to apply for such courses in the early stages of your final year if you are also applying for financial support, yet you cannot be sure that you will get the necessary class of degree until you have completed your course. Many graduates end up taking a year out before beginning further study because they have missed the deadlines, but this can be a good thing, as it gives you the chance to earn some money and catch up financially, as well as giving you some useful work experience. Of course, if you intend to finance your own higher degree, you will have more flexibility about when you apply. The answer is to consider this possibility as early as possible, certainly by the beginning of your final year. In the same way that undergraduates are reluctant to forecast their final results, they are also reticent about suggesting that they might want to undertake further study, feeling that they might not be up to the standard required. Try not to be too modest: your personal tutor is there to advise you on all aspects of your academic career and will be supportive of your interest in studying beyond your degree.

It is impossible to say whether it will be worth your while financially to undertake a higher degree. In some careers, it is considered essential that you have worked beyond degree level, in other areas it makes no difference. Most graduates who undertake a higher degree do so because they have a passionate interest in one field of study, and so they do an MA or a PhD with only one eye on the job market, happy to explore their career options once they have completed their research. If you do decide to apply to extend your university life beyond your degree, you will have to produce a research proposal of some sort and, again, your department and Careers Advisory Service will be able to help you. Your proposal might be brief, confined to the pages of a form similar to a job application form, or it might be a more extended piece of work, designed to test the feasibility of your proposed project. There are books available to help you in this process, but there are some guidelines that are worth keeping in mind, regardless of the form that your research proposal takes:

Do:
- Ensure that you have the timing right: know exactly when each stage of your application is due to be completed.
- Fill out every form that is sent to you, completely and in the required format.
- Leave yourself more time than you ever thought possible to fill out the forms, collect references and so on.
- Inform your referees and potential supervisor of your intentions and each step that you take.
- Give a copy of the completed forms to each of your referees and make sure that they are aware of the time frame within which you are working.
- Network as widely as you can: you might find useful funding opportunities in the least expected places.
- Check (on the Internet and elsewhere) the details of the funding body to which you are applying: you might discover that they favour certain types of project, or that they have a 'frequently asked questions' (FAQs) section on their website.

- Make sure that you are aware of, and mention, every current publication that might have a bearing on your research.
- Try to show originality in your proposal: how will your work add to the sum of knowledge in your area?

Do not:
- Forget to have a backup plan: What will you do if your application is unsuccessful?
- Ignore any of the options available to you, however remote they seem at first glance.
- Assume that everyone who is involved in your application is as enthusiastic, or as efficient, as you are.
- Just see the application process as a form-filling exercise: it is a chance for you to see how viable your proposed research is when it is fleshed out.
- Assume that the panel making a decision on your proposal or application is as informed as you are: use accessible language and be clear about what you intend to achieve.
- See the process as a 'one-off': keep your notes on file for future use.
- Be hesitant about contacting the funding body if you are unsure about any of the instructions that you have been given.
- Ignore the help that is on offer from your department and Careers Advisory Service.
- Worry too much about your proposal once it has been submitted: get on with other projects whilst you await a decision.
- Expect a swift response: it will be some time before you discover whether you have been successful.

You will inevitably spend some of your time during your last year at university thinking about the future. Even if you came to university with a fairly clear idea about your future career, you will want to consider whether your original plans still hold up after the experience of being an undergraduate, and you will be aware that time is moving inexorably towards a new beginning. However, the pressure of the final year of studying may leave you with little opportunity to do more than think about the future. Then you graduate and suddenly you are faced with the prospect of putting the theory into practice. You might decide to continue with your studies, or to undertake a work placement of some sort so as to decide where you want to work in the future, but for most graduates their preferred option is to try to get a job, and it is to this aspect of managing your life as a graduate that we will now turn.

Spot guide

The key points to remember from this chapter:

- make sure that you are clear about the timing and requirements of assessed coursework and examinations
- begin to plan your revision well before the examinations
- prepare a revision timetable and try to stick to it, but allow for some flexibility
- vary the revision techniques that you use so as to maximise their effect
- attend a study skills course if you need extra help with your examination technique
- join revision groups, or arrange one for yourself, if you find this helpful
- discover the best examination technique for you and stick with it
- practise relaxation techniques before you face the examinations
- practise examination essays, at least in plan form, as part of your revision
- in the examination, leave yourself enough time to plan each answer and check your work thoroughly
- explore all your postgraduate options as your undergraduate course progresses
- remain open to all the options that might be available to you once you have graduated

9 Life after your Degree

Troubleshooting guide

Use this chapter for help in the following areas:

- if you have not yet developed a career strategy
- if you are unsure of the value of your vacation jobs or your work or study placement
- if you need help in seeing the commercial value of the work you have done at university
- if you are not sure how to find out about the careers that might be available to you once you graduate
- if you have little experience in researching the job market
- if you are anxious about making direct contact with potential employers
- if you need advice about completing application forms
- if you do not have an effective or up-to-date CV
- if you need help with your interview technique

▶ Your career strategy

During your degree course you will rightly be spending the majority of your time working towards your degree, and this might leave you with little chance to consider the wider career implications of what you are doing, yet your degree will form only one part of your overall career strategy. Even if you do not have a clear idea of where you will end up, you can begin to work towards your career as you study. Many aspects of your life as an under-graduate can be used towards making you an attractive proposition to an employer, and it is a good idea to keep a file on your activities with a view to creating a persuasive CV once you begin to look for a job. Although this may not be your top priority in the early stages of your degree course, you will find it easier to apply for jobs, and perform well at interview, if you have done some groundwork as you progress through your degree course. It is surprisingly difficult to remember everything that you have done once you are faced with the prospect of having to prepare your first CV, so early preparation will help. There are several areas of your time at university that might be included in your 'career file':

- *Vacation and part-time jobs:* working in a fast-food chain may not seem to you to be the most inspiring work, but the experience will allow you to show that you have acquired marketable skills, such as working as a member of a team, often under pressure and with a strong element of customer service. No job is too lowly to be included in your career file, as each new experience will have given you skills that you can highlight on your CV. If you make a note at the time of the tasks that you have undertaken, you will be ready to talk persuasively at interview about what you have gained from your part-time work as an undergraduate. Of course, you do not have to ignore your possible career prospects just because you have to earn money. It might be easy to get a job in a fast-food chain or a local pub or club, but, as was explored in Chapter 6, you might be better paid working in other areas, such as in a call centre or an office. The vacations also offer you the chance to take on more challenging work, perhaps related to the career that you hope to enter once you graduate, and it is useful to be able to mention all your part-time work in your CV but then to focus in some detail upon one really interesting job.

The advantage of creating a career file as you go along is that you will not forget the minor details of a job: these are often the most impressive aspects from the point of view of a prospective employer. It may be, for example, that you spent six weeks working behind the bar of your local pub: but you might easily have forgotten two years later that you also organised the local pub quiz night for charity. This may have been only a very minor part of your overall job, but it will allow you to demonstrate to an employer that you have begun to develop organisational skills, experience in PR and leadership qualities. Once you begin to create a career file, you may find yourself being more selective about the work that you do. Although you will still need to earn money and might not be faced with a great choice of jobs, you will be aware that the job that you did in your last vacation gave you teamworking skills, so you now need to get a job that will show your logistical, managerial or interpersonal skills. In this way, you will still earn the money that you need, but you will also be building a portfolio of transferable skills.

- *Work placements:* These schemes are obviously a good chance to acquire work-related skills. Again, you may well forget some of the details of what you have achieved by the time you graduate, so it is worth making quite detailed notes of the skills you acquired and how you used them. It is also a good idea to get a copy of the report made on you by the employer, if this is possible. The report given to your university may be confidential, but this does not prevent you from asking directly for a reference, if you think that you have worked well. If your placement was for studying rather than work experience, you will still have been involved in new ways of working, perhaps in a different culture, and this offers you another opportunity to show off your flexibility and range of study and work skills.

Employers often use work and study placements as easy talking points at interview. They know that they are on safe ground when they ask you questions about something that you must know all about, but some graduates answer questions about their work placements in monosyllabic answers, as if they are afraid to say too much or perhaps because they did not really enjoy the experience. Whether you found your placement a pleasure or a pain, make sure that, as soon as possible after the event, you write down a succinct account of what you have done and what you have achieved. No employer is going to want to hear a blow by blow account of every day that you spent on placement, but if you have made notes at the time, you can rehearse your account before your interview, remembering to stress the good points, the positive aspects of the placement and the skills you acquired in the process.

- *Joint projects:* It is highly unlikely that you will have undertaken the whole of your degree course in isolation. At the very least you will have been part of a team in a seminar situation. If you take the time to think about it, you will find that other aspects of your undergraduate experience also involved teamwork: perhaps you were on a committee for a club or society, or maybe you worked on a team-based project during part of your course. You need to analyse your role in these joint projects: Are you a natural leader or a supportive member of the team? Did you chair meetings (even informal discussion meetings about a seminar paper) or perhaps organise the material for a formal presentation? Did you have to represent your team at any point? Did you generate discussion, suggest solutions or articulate collective ideas? Identifying these aspects of your teamworking experience will be useful when you come to prepare your CV.

It is a common misconception that employers are just looking for the most qualified person for a job. In fact, any organisation, commercial or otherwise, is simply an extended team and employers are looking to employ someone who will fit into that team. They can always train you: this is usually far cheaper than having to readvertise the position and go through the whole selection process again because they have employed someone who cannot work as a constructive member of their team.

- *Dissertations:* If you have produced a dissertation as part of your degree you will probably have viewed it as just another module to be completed on your course: in reality, it is the perfect chance to prove to prospective employers that you have the personal qualities they need. In producing your dissertation, you have shown that you can work with a minimal level of supervision, can think independently about ideas and concepts and have a creative flair. You will also be able to prove that you have excellent time management skills. You might know that you produced the whole thing at the last minute in a flat spin, but the employer does not know that, and the fact that you did achieve the necessary result within a stipulated time period is all that matters now.

As with work and study placements, employers like to ask graduates about their dissertations at interview, and you are also likely to have prompted this response by highlighting your dissertation on your CV, especially if it is relevant to the job for which you are applying. Again, you do not need to go into a rambling discussion of the experience if you are asked about your dissertation. Prepare your answer in advance, finding ways in which you can describe your dissertation so that anyone can understand what you have done, and taking the opportunity to stress the skills that you acquired in the process. You do not have to be too strait-laced about this: it is perfectly acceptable to smile about any difficulties that you encountered, but make sure that your account is upbeat and positive. One of the main advantages of having done a placement or dissertation during your degree is that you can be fairly sure that the interviewer will ask about them and so you have, to some extent, taken control of the interview in advance. You will have prepared answers to one or two of the questions and so will be able to concentrate on the rest of the interview in a more productive way.

- *Presentations:* As an increasingly popular part of degree programmes, you are likely to have given at least one presentation at university: make the most of it. Once you have given the presentation, make a note for your career file of what went right and, as importantly, what went wrong and how you overcame any problems. One of the questions often asked at interview is how you have overcome any difficulties in the past. If you are able to explain how you faced up to and overcame a problem with a presentation, you can answer the question in a way that is both honest and positive.

Another advantage of making notes after you have given a presentation, even if it is a minor presentation to your seminar group, is that you will be reminded of how to do it if you are asked to give a presentation as part of the selection procedure for a job. This form of evaluation is on the increase, yet it can be difficult to remember how to present well if you have not done it for some time. Although you will have thought at the time that you would always remember the experience, it is easy to forget that you spoke too quickly, ran over time or stood in front of your visual display. Referring back to the notes in your career file will reassure you that you can give an impressive presentation to your prospective employer.

- *Research:* You might not think that you have done any independent research during your degree, but you have, even if it was under the guidance of a tutor, so make a note in your career file of what you learnt from the experience. If, for example, you had to undertake a case study, find material in a series of journals in order to support your hypothesis or bring your viewpoint to bear upon established research, you will be able to talk enthusiastically about the process. You will want to stress the fact that you were working to a deadline, that you had to work largely unsupervised and that you were able to produce a new hypothesis, supported by relevant material.

This may sound obvious to you, given that you have had to produce essays and perhaps more extended pieces of work throughout your degree course, but employers are not simply looking for graduates: they are looking for employees who can analyse the experience of being an undergraduate, identify the skills that they have acquired and articulate their ideas and hopes for their future development.

▶ Breaking into the career market

It is an often publicised fact that the vast majority of vacancies are not advertised: the figure is sometimes put as high as 80 per cent. This leaves you with a dilemma: you know that the jobs are out there somewhere, but are not sure exactly which one you want or how to get at it. The first thing to do is to carry out some research. You will never be able to find out about every job that you might like to do, but your Careers Advisory Service will be able to work through the possibilities with you, administering personality and aptitude tests to help you to narrow down the options. If a career management module formed part of your degree, you will have had the chance to do extensive research into the job market well before you graduate.

Once you have decided upon an area, or more probably several areas, that interest you, you are still left with the problem of breaking into the job market. There are several ways in which you can tackle this, and using a combination of all of these approaches will give you the best chance of landing yourself the right job.

Careers fairs

You will have noticed the signs around the university advertising these and it is a good idea to browse around them in the early stages of your time at university. When you reach the stage of deciding to attend a fair to look more seriously for a job, remember that you are making judgements about the organisations that are at the fair, as well as allowing them to assess you as a potential employee. Make sure that you gather as much information as you can in this relatively informal setting, but keep an eye on the people who are there to represent the organisation. If they seem negative, rather too pushy for your liking or, as can sometimes happen, just look downright miserable, take this as a reflection of the organisation for whom they are working. In the same way that you are judging them, they will be assessing you. Even if you are only browsing around with the intention of asking some fairly general questions, make sure that you look smart, alert and keen to work. Seeing an undergraduate looking half asleep and in scruffy clothes will not inspire them, and general discussions can quickly turn into informal interviews on the spot, so prepare something to say about yourself so that the selling can start on a positive note.

Departmental information

You may find that your department takes only a limited interest in your job hunt, but it is more probable that it has one member of staff who is assigned to look after the career prospects of its undergraduates. Universities are under pressure to achieve good employment outcomes for their graduates and so it is increasingly the case that departments, schools and faculties pool their resources and data in order to help graduates into jobs. Departments sometimes hold information about the career destinations of past graduates and this can be an easy way of beginning your research. It may even be possible for you to make contact directly with past graduates who have successfully entered a career area in which you have an interest. As with so much else, your departmental secretary will be able to point you in the right direction.

Newspapers

These are an obvious place to begin your job hunt, but be as creative as you can in your searching. If, for example, you notice that a particular organisation is placing several adverts for different positions, you can be reasonably sure that they are running a recruitment drive and it will be worth your while to contact them in case they are extending their recruitment to an area that is of interest to you. Local free papers are a good source of information, as are specialist journals in your field, particularly if you are looking for work in Social Science. Again, do not just take the information at face value: if an organisation looks interesting, give them a call.

The Internet

This is an increasingly accessible and popular source of information about careers and job vacancies and it is one to which you will turn early in your search. Make sure that you are targeted in your approach, or you might waste hours looking at sites that are of only marginal use to you, or simply logging on to the sites that are run by job agencies, where a direct approach to employers might be more productive. Again, if you reach the site of an organisation that interests you, use the Internet to find out as much as you can about the organisation and then contact them directly.

Job agencies

There are many very good job agencies, and some that will be useless to you, either because they do not specialise in your field of interest or because they are overloaded with candidates and short of vacancies to offer them. Be selective: talk to your fellow students to find out which are the best agencies to contact and then take control of the situation. If they want to produce a CV for you, make sure that you have the final say on its content and presentation. If they want to send you for an interview, make absolutely certain that you know where they are sending you and what the job on offer entails. The exception to this note of caution is probably temporary job agencies, which can be a useful source of work whilst you decide where to go next. If you can develop a good relationship with your agency, you will be in a position to be selective about the work that you get offered, allowing you to scout around the job market whilst getting paid.

Radio

Although this has never become a major source of information about job vacancies, local radio stations can be handy for giving you an insight into the job market by running features on local employers, so it should not be ignored entirely if you have the time to listen.

Networking

A very effective way to carry out your job search, but it will take some work. Initially, you might feel that you have nobody to network with, but remain open to possibilities. If you have done vacation work or a work or study placement, make sure that you keep in touch with those with whom you worked. If an organisation produces an internal vacancies bulletin, for example, try to arrange to get a copy of it sent to you from your former work colleagues. If you discover that friends at university have contacts within organisations that are of interest to you, be shameless about using them. It is also a good idea to create a career network before you graduate: this consists of a group of students who can remain in contact via email in order to pass on information about jobs and career opportunities once you have all graduated. You may have seen these people regularly at university, but once you leave you can lose contact with surprising ease. If you set up this fairly formal means of networking whilst you are all still together, you will give yourself the best chance of working as an effective networking group in the future; these groups can last for years, as you all progress into new areas of your careers.

Direct contact

This is the most challenging, but also the most effective way to get into a career. By contacting organisations direct you will be getting behind the advertised job market into what is often called the hidden job market, where jobs vacancies are filled by word of mouth rather than by a formal recruitment procedure. You might be making 'warm calls', that is, contacting an organisation because you have noticed that it is recruiting, or 'cold calls', where you will be making contact with an organisation just because you might like to work for it, without any knowledge of whether it is recruiting or not. If the organisation has not yet advertised a vacancy that has just arisen, you will be streets ahead of the opposition. Making direct contact is an efficient use of your time and will be necessary even if you are responding to an advert: in this case, you will need to know whether the vacancy still exists (this can save you hours of wasted time), whether you can fill their requirements and whether the organisation is one that suits you. There are techniques to this approach that you will need to master:

- Do the research: if you have heard of an organisation that interests you, find out as much as you can about it, via a website or by getting hold of a company brochure.
- Prepare your paperwork in advance: before you telephone, have your CV in front of you, a list of questions that you want to ask and a pen and paper ready to take notes. Be ready for your enquiry to turn into an

informal telephone interview. If you realise that there are new questions that you can ask in future calls, add them to your list as you go along. You will probably find that, by the end of the first three calls, your 'script' is twice as long as it was at the outset.

- Have a series of telephone calls arranged before you begin: make a list of a dozen organisations that appeal to you and then brace yourself to make all the calls in one day.

- Before you make the calls, make sure that you are as ready as you can be, with no possibility of interruptions. Sit at a table if possible and dress as if you were actually meeting the people on the end of the telephone. This may sound odd, but if you are sitting slouched in an armchair dressed in your scruffiest clothes, your voice will automatically sound less sharp and you will be less ready to cope with any searching questions that you are asked.

- Do not be disappointed if you cannot get through to the human resources department on your first try: receptionists can be an invaluable source of information that is not readily available elsewhere, so keep them talking about the organisation if you can. You can always call back another time and try again if you cannot get through to the right department on your first go.

- Begin with your least favoured option and work up. You might find that on your first call your mouth goes dry and you forget what you wanted to say. It will not matter if your first call is a disaster: you have plenty more options in front of you. You will also be amazed at how quickly you become adept at this exercise. I have seen students who were quivering wrecks on the first call become dynamic salespeople by the third.

- If you suspect that the first call is going to be a nightmare, when you might forget what you wanted to say or just dry up altogether, dial 141 (so that your number cannot be traced) before you make the call and, if it all goes wrong, just put the telephone down. They will never know who was calling them, and you can try again later when you become more expert.

- As you probably did with your revising, offer yourself incentives: a break after the first two calls, a chocolate bar after the next two and so on. It sounds simple, but you need to impose some structure on the process if you are to keep yourself going.

- Be ready to enjoy yourself. Although this exercise can be terrifying in prospect, comfort yourself with the fact that it is probably the best way for you to get a job, and you will find that, with practice, it can be a satisfying and enjoyable process.

- Avoid the temptation to be negative. If an organisation has no vacancies at the moment, this does not mean that they will not have any jobs on offer next week. If you can get a conversation going and arrange to send them your CV, they can get back to you when an opportunity arises: this really does happen. It is expensive for an organisation to recruit new staff: if your details are on file it is more cost effective for them to come back to you direct when a vacancy arises.

- See this as a fact-finding mission. This exercise is as much about you exploring what they have to offer as it is about you being vetted by them. If the receptionist is rude and the manager is unhelpful and unsure about what they might have on offer, you might decide that you are not interested in them, which will save you the trouble of applying to them when they do advertise vacancies.

- Try to explore every possible avenue. If you really like the sound of an organisation and your feelings are confirmed in your telephone conversation, be ready to ask to have a meeting with a manager or the human resources department, in case they have any vacancies in the future. Be prepared also, if you are in a position to do this, to offer yourself for a placement, perhaps shadowing a member of staff or working on a project just to gain some experience in the field: this is obviously a tempting prospect for any organisation. If they are unlikely to have any vacancies in the foreseeable future, you could ask whether they know of any similar organisations in the area that are recruiting, but only ask about this if you feel that you have reached a dead end.

- Have a script ready: you can abandon it to some extent if the telephone call becomes more of a real conversation, but be ready with your questions and your sales pitch. Although your line of questioning will vary according to the organisation that you are calling and the experience that you are offering them, there are some general questions that you are likely to want to ask:
  - Hello, my name is . . . and I am a graduate from . . . (I have noticed that you are currently recruiting.) I am ringing to ask whether you have any vacancies at the moment. I am interested in working in. . . .
  - (If they do not have any vacancies.) Could you tell me where you usually advertise your vacancies?
  - Could you tell me something about your organisation? I notice that you work in the area of . . . and I am interested in working in this area, as my degree course covered some aspects of this.
  - Do you have a graduate training programme? When do you usually recruit for this?
  - Do you ever run shadowing or career experience schemes? I am particularly keen to work for your organisation and would be happy to

be involved in such a scheme. Perhaps I could come and discuss the possibility with you?
 – Perhaps I could send you my CV, so that you can keep it on file?

You will find your own way to ask these questions and there will be more that you will want to add as you become more confident about what you are doing. In an ideal scenario, by the end of the call you will have made sure that you have the name of the person with whom you were speaking and you will have agreed to send them your CV, or have arranged a meeting to discuss the possibilities that might be open to you. You will also have gathered enough information about the organisation (perhaps by asking them to send you their company brochure) to make your CV as targeted as possible.

If you decide to be proactive about breaking into a career when you graduate, telephone calls will form the mainstay of your job search. It is not always easy to begin with, but it does get easier and it does produce results.

▶ Conquering the paperwork

Getting into the right job often seems to involve mountains of paperwork. You will need to be organised before you begin. Keep a file on each organisation that you have approached, so that you can refer back to the notes that you made during the telephone call, the application form that you filled in and the CV that you sent. Keeping your records up to date need not be a chore: in reality, you will find it reassuring as it imposes some structure on what can be a relatively unstructured period of your life. When you become anxious about your chances of getting a job, you can look into your files and remind yourself that you are doing everything that you can do towards that end, and this is a comfort if things seem to be moving too slowly. There are books available that will help you in the process of filling out application forms and writing covering letters, so a few reminders here will suffice:

- When you fill out an application form, photocopy the form first and fill it out perfectly before you write on the original.
- Fill out the application form exactly as you are asked to do, trying not to leave any sections blank and avoiding the temptation to write 'refer to CV' anywhere.
- Get someone to check your draft version before you complete the original.
- If you are filling out an application form on-line, save it and go back to check it the next day before sending it off, just in case you have missed anything.

- If you find yourself filling out a very long application form, with a series of unexpected questions at the end, you are probably facing a 'competence' application form, one that aims to test your aptitude and personality as well as gathering information about you. This need not be a problem: these forms often replace the first interview stage of the recruitment process, so they can work in your favour.

- Although you will need to target every application form (and letter and CV) to the job for which you are applying, you can usefully use the information on one to create another, so keep copies of all your paperwork so as to save yourself time later.

- Each document that you produce should be sufficient to stand alone as part of your application. The human resources department might photocopy only your application form, or only your CV, for the interview panel, so it does not matter if you repeat yourself to some extent, perhaps by highlighting the best points from your CV in your covering letter.

- Remember that your paperwork will be photocopied, so make it clear and write in black ink so that it is legible even if it is photocopied several times.

Although you are likely to be asked to complete an application form at some stage of the recruitment process, this is not necessarily the principal document in your job search. If you succeed in your telephone calls, you will probably be asked to send your CV to an organisation. In some cases, successful candidates are asked to complete an application form only after they have been interviewed, just to satisfy the protocol of the organisation concerned. Your CV is going to be vital to you.

You will already have some idea of what to include in your CV from your career file, where you have gathered information about your impressive skills base and achievements that you want to highlight for an employer. However, before you begin to write anything down, you need to take a step back and consider what you want your CV to do for you. You are trying to sell yourself to an employer, and, like any successful marketing strategy, you need to know as much as you can about the sales situation before you begin. There are three main points to bear in mind:

1. *Know who are.* That is, know who you are from the point of view of employment. What are you selling? What are your unique selling points?

2. *Know where you want to be.* Even if you are applying for a vacancy that has been advertised, you will not have enough information from an advert to make the best sales pitch. You will need to make a telephone call to find out more about the vacancy and the organisation.

3. *Know what they want.* You can usually get hold of a copy of a full job description and person specification if you contact the organisation, and this will give you essential clues about how to target your CV and application form. If you check their website or get a copy of their company brochure or marketing material, you can learn about the culture of the organisation, and so work out what sort of person they are likely to employ.

At every stage in this process of learning about your prospective employer, remember that you are free to pull out. You have not yet even begun to write your CV or fill out an application form, so if your instinct is telling you that this is not the right company for you, trust it and move ahead with your next prospect.

If the organisation is still one to which you want to apply once you have done the initial research, you will want to begin to prepare your CV. Remember that your CV is your sales pitch, so you have to make each word count, and this is easier to do if you keep these five points in mind:

1. *Clarity:* never assume that the prospective employer will be an expert in your field. If you want to highlight your dissertation in your CV, make sure that you describe it in terms that the lay person can understand. If you have attended any professional development courses, make it quite clear what was involved and what relevant skills you acquired.
2. *Focus:* it is often said that an employer will study a CV for no more than 90 seconds before deciding whether to put it on the 'yes', 'no' or 'maybe' pile. In some situations, this is a generous estimate of how long an employer will take, so you need to make sure that every line of your CV makes the employer want to keep reading.
3. *Relevance:* to each job for which you are applying. You will not be able to create one CV to fit every vacancy. Although there will be some overlap, you must make sure that you highlight those points that are most relevant to each employer. Even if you are applying for two jobs with the same job title, one person specification might foreground skills that are only mentioned in passing in another. At all stages, you have to pass the 'so what' test. When you review your CV, decide whether at any point the employer is likely to say 'so what?' If this is the case, remove or downgrade the section that is not working.
4. *Interest:* that is, interest to the employer. You may feel justly proud of your IT proficiency, but if the job for which you are applying involves very little IT, you will need to include only a brief mention of these skills, leaving more space for those selling points that are of more interest to the employer. You need not ignore the experience that you have gained

outside your degree programme. If you believe that your prospective employer will be interested in your time spent scuba diving on the Great Barrier Reef, include it under your hobbies and interests and be ready to make it a talking point at interview.

5. *The whole truth?:* the days when you could just flannel your way through a CV and hope for the best are long gone. You are a graduate, with an interesting and relevant course of study to talk about at interview and a skills base that will be impressive enough in itself without the need for you to embroider the truth. Embellishing your CV beyond the bounds that you can support at interview is a waste of your time and energy. If you claim on your CV that you have a good knowledge of German, for example, even though you last spoke German at GCSE, you will spend your time at interview anxiously waiting for them to ask you to converse in German, rather than using your energy to focus on framing impressive answers to the questions that you are being asked. For most candidates, the problem is reversed. If you are concerned that you have something to say that you feel will not impress the employer (perhaps you failed an A level, or have a medical condition that concerns you), you are likely to overemphasise this on your CV because you want to be upfront and get it out of the way before you get to interview. The answer here is to get the balance right. You need to be truthful, but there is no point in overly highlighting what you consider to be a negative point, as the employer is unlikely to worry about it as much as you do.

The difficulty for most graduates seems to be false modesty. They tend to believe that they have nothing more than their degree to offer, when in fact they have an impressive range of skills and experience that will make them attractive to any employer, as long as they can be persuaded to mention them. If you find yourself staring at a blank piece of paper, feeling that you have nothing much to say and very little to offer, enlist the help of friends and family, who will be happy to remind you of just how employable you are. On a similar note, when you have a completed your CV, put a copy of it on the fridge door, so that you remind yourself of how marketable you are every time you see it. We tend to forget our good points all too quickly, and seeing yourself in print in this way can be a lasting confidence boost as you go through the process of breaking into the career market.

Once you have worked through these general aspects of creating a CV and have all the information to hand to help you to target your CV to the job for which you are applying, you are ready to write the CV. The format of your CV may take several forms, and you will find that everyone whom you ask for guidance will have different advice to offer. In the end, you will have to decide on the best format for you, but there are two general points to remember.

Firstly, try to create a CV that is two pages long: this is the usual length for a CV, and making it longer or shorter will suggest either that you cannot be concise or that you have too little to say about yourself. Secondly, keep a copy of each CV that you produce. You will soon find that you have a 'master CV' that is perhaps three or four pages long, from which you can pick the most relevant sections for each position for which you are applying.

Although you will work within the most effective format for you, the CV outlined below, for the student who has appeared throughout this book, will get you started. She is applying for a place on a graduate trainee programme within a marketing firm. The job description includes arranging marketing meetings, helping to design stands for trade fairs and working as a member of the creative team for product launches. She has spoken to the organisation and has a copy of the company brochure, the job description and the person specification, so she is in a good position to target her CV to both the organisation and the position for which she is applying.

Curriculum Vitae
Sarah Elizabeth Carter

24 Cheyne Close, Bristol BS2 8QA
Tel: 0256 443 5678; mobile: 07651 204 667

An English graduate with experience in the field of marketing. A team player with excellent communication skills and a keen commercial awareness.

Key Skills and Experience

Marketing: In my second year at university I spent a six-week career placement with a PR and marketing firm, gaining valuable insight into the field of marketing.

Communication: I have experience of dealing with clients by telephone, letter and in person. As chairperson of my university debating society, I was given the opportunity to develop a range of communication skills.

Continued

Teamwork: Throughout my time at university I worked part time as a member of a small team in a busy restaurant. I had to work effectively under pressure and meet deadlines whilst maintaining a high quality of service.

Organisation: I am a highly organised individual, and this was vital to the successful completion of my dissertation, which was delivered on time and to the specified requirements and for which I gained a First Class mark.

Information Technology: I have undertaken courses in Office 2000, Front Page and PowerPoint. I am keen to continue to develop my IT skills in the workplace.

Education

1999–2002: Honours Degree (2:1) in English with modules also successfully completed in History and Sociology. My dissertation, entitled 'Communication in the Modern Workplace' formed an important part of my degree course.

1997–1999: A levels gained in English (A), History (A) and Law (D).

GCSEs gained in ten subjects, including English, Mathematics, ICT, French and German.

Professional Development

Courses undertaken in Office 2000, Front Page and PowerPoint. I have a working knowledge of a variety of design packages and some experience of accounting software.

As part of my work placement with Interscan PR and Marketing, I attended a course entitled 'Effective Communication in Marketing'.

I received in-house training in Customer Care during my vacation work.

Career History

2002 to present: Since graduating I have worked on a voluntary basis for a local charity. My role has included:
- arranging public information events
- providing administrative support for a team of six
- organising fund-raising activities

Continued

2001: Six-week work placement with Interscan, a PR and marketing firm concerned with the launch of IT packages and the provision of software support. My role included:

- arranging marketing meetings for up to 20 members of staff
- undertaking statistical analysis of market research data
- reviewing the in-house newsletter and making recommendations for improvement

1999 to 2002: Part-time vacation work with Chortles Bistro, developing my role from kitchen assistant to section leader. My role included:

- maintaining excellent customer satisfaction with the service in the bistro
- mentoring new staff
- arranging staffing schedules and managing a section within the restaurant

Additional Information

Whilst at university I was chairperson of the University Debating Society and was involved in promoting the university to prospective students on guided tours.

I am currently attending a course in Business and Conversational French.

I hold a first aid certificate.

I am physically fit and have a current driving licence.

My interests include reading (I particularly enjoy political biographies), sport (at school I swam at competition level) and cinema (I am a member of my local film appreciation society).

References are available on request

As you can see, Sarah has made the most of everything that she has ever done. She has targeted her CV to the company and provided plenty of useful starting points for discussion at interview. She probably began by thinking that she did not have much to say on a CV: she has now found that she has difficulty squeezing everything into two A4 pages. She will have left out some information that she thinks is less relevant to this job, but will have kept it on file ready for use later on.

▶ Interviews

You will find that your Careers Advisory Service is a useful source of help and guidance when you are preparing to be interviewed. You will also find it helpful to practise your interview technique with your friends, perhaps on a reciprocal basis. Each interview will be different. You will attend a first interview, which might be quite brief, then second (or third) interviews which will be more demanding. You might be interviewed by a single manager or a panel of interviewers; you might be asked to give a presentation. Although these interview settings present differing challenges, there are some key points that will help you to succeed, whatever the interview situation:

* Make absolutely certain that you are sure of the logistics of the interview: timing, location, travel arrangements and the probable length of the interview.
* Contact the organisation if you are anxious about what to expect, such as whether it is to be a panel interview, or whether there will be group activities. If you have been asked to give a presentation, ring to confirm that you have got all the details correct, such as the time allowed to you, the size of the room and the audience, and whether or not you will be expected to use visual aids.
* Take all your application paperwork with you, in case you need to refer to it, and include any other paperwork that you might like to present at interview if you get the chance, such as references from a work placement or the report on your dissertation.
* Use your nerves: it is fine to be nervous, this will keep you sharp and focused, but employ the examination techniques that were discussed in Chapter 8 so that you can use your nerves positively.
* See the selection process as beginning as soon as you walk in the door and not ending until you are safely on your way home. You will be judged on whether you are on time, how well you interact with the staff whom you meet, how successfully you can perform in a team situation and how open and responsive you are throughout your time with the organisation.
* When you enter the interview room, make eye contact and shake hands firmly with the interviewer or with each member of the interview panel.
* Prepare some answers in advance. You will not want to come across as if you are reading from a prepared script, but you can reasonably assume that some typical questions are likely to be asked and, if you have some idea of how you will answer them, you can conserve your energy ready for the unexpected or more challenging questions. You can safely assume

that the interview will begin with a question designed to put you at your ease (Did you find us easily? How was your journey?), but it will soon move on to more open conversational gambits, such as 'Tell us something about yourself' (they do not want your life story: you can prepare a summary of your career and academic achievements in advance and so be ready for this one). Some questions come up time and time again, such as 'Tell us about your weaknesses/strengths'. Again, you can prepare the outline answer in advance, making sure that you highlight your strengths and have an example ready to demonstrate them.

- Even if you are uncertain of what you might be asked, you can prepare some useful 'all purpose' examples. Using your CV as a prompt, try to remember a time when you faced a difficult situation and show how you overcame it. Think of the achievement of which you are most proud and practise summarising it. Identify which of your experiences is most relevant to the position for which you are applying and be ready to use it.

- If, at the close of the interview, you are asked if you have any questions, be succinct and positive; try to avoid mentioning money at the first interview.

Once you have completed the interview, try to forget about it. Move on to your next application: there is no point in wasting time worrying about the outcome when you could be expanding your options. If you are unsuccessful, pluck up the courage to ring and ask why you were not selected: it is unlikely that it had much to do with your performance at interview; it is more probable that they found somebody with more relevant and specific experience or qualifications, or that they appointed an internal candidate. I have heard of cases where unsuccessful candidates made this call, only to find that the successful candidate had not taken up the job and they were offered it themselves instead. It is certainly worth making the call.

As you manoeuvre your way through the minefield of job hunting, you will experience a range of emotions: excitement, hope, perhaps disappointment and, finally, the thrill of succeeding in getting a job. Whilst you are researching the career market, applying for jobs and attending interviews, remember that you are a graduate: you have already managed your degree effectively and have succeeded in gaining a world-class qualification; you are going to be a valuable asset to any organisation lucky enough to get you. In the years to come you will recognise that managing your degree was just the start of a lifelong process: by taking a proactive approach to the management of your degree, you will have gained skills and experience that will help you as you progress in your career. You will be able to look back on your time as an undergraduate as not just an enjoyable period of your life, but as the best start that you could have given yourself in becoming the person who you want to be. Good luck!

Spot guide

The key points to remember from this chapter:

- everything that you have done whilst at university will be useful to you in your search for the right job
- make a career file, in which you can gather information about your skills and achievements as you go along
- attend the Careers Fairs at your university, both to gather information and make contact with potential employers
- use as many sources of information as possible in your search for a career break
- network with other students and keep the network going once you have graduated
- making direct contact with organisations is the most effective way to move ahead in your job search
- practise your telephone technique until you become an effective salesperson for what you have to offer
- master the paperwork, including application forms, letters and CVs
- see your CV as your main sales pitch and work on it as you progress, targeting it to each new vacancy
- practise your interview technique until you have perfected it
- use your Careers Advisory Service to the full
- explore every career possibility thoroughly
- try to impose some structure on your job search, and do not give up: you are getting better all the time!

Recommended Reading

Coombes, H. *Research Using IT* (Basingstoke: Palgrave Macmillan, 2001)

Cottrell, S. *The Study Skills Handbook* (Basingstoke: Macmillan – now Palgrave Macmillan, 1999)

Greetham, B. *How to Write Better Essays* (Basingstoke: Palgrave Macmillan, 2001)

Peck, J. and Coyle, M. *The Student's Guide to Writing* (Basingstoke: Macmillan – now Palgrave Macmillan, 1999)

Rose, J. *The Mature Student's Guide to Writing* (Basingstoke: Palgrave Macmillan, 2001)

van Emden, J. and Becker, L. *Effective Communication for Arts and Humanities Students* (Basingstoke: Palgrave Macmillan, 2003)

Index